Gooseberry patch

From our Kitchen to Yours

Go-To Recipes For a

13x9 Pan

Table of Contents

Dedication

For every cook who wants to make easy and delicious recipes for their family & friends using their favorite 13x9 pan.

....

Appreciation

Thanks to everyone who shared their delightful and delicious recipes with us!

....

Gooseberry Patch
An imprint of Globe Pequot
64 S. Main Street
Essex, CT 06426

www.gooseberrypatch.com
1•800•854•6673

Copyright © 2023, Gooseberry Patch
978-1-62093-545-3

Welcome

Dear Friends,

There is nothing more satisfying than preparing tasty dishes for your family & friends for every meal of the day. Using your much-loved 13 x 9-inch pan can make the process even easier and clean-up is a breeze!

Go-To Recipes for a 13x9 Pan is the perfect cookbook that uses that favorite 13x9 pan that has become a cook's best friend. Whether you are looking for a delightful breakfast meal, a quick snack or sandwich, a comfort-food casserole or a sweet dessert, you'll find it in this book of tried & true recipes from **Gooseberry Patch.**

Inside this book you'll find breakfast and bread recipes like Buttermilk Cinnamon Rolls (page 44) and Rise & Shine Breakfast Pizza (page 56). You'll love the French Toast with Praline Sauce (page 58) for that special Sunday brunch. Need a tasty snack? Mini Ham Balls (page 62) are an all-time favorite! Serve some Cheesy Chile Artichoke Dip (page 68) along with them for a great appetizer combo. Everyone needs a little comfort food once in awhile. Nothing could be better than a No-Fuss Chicken Dinner (page 142) or easy-to-make Cranberry Meatloaves (Page 152). Need a little more spice? Serve Garlicky Baked Shrimp (page 138) or Baked Chicken Chimichangas (page 144). There is always room for a sweet treat, and making it in a 13x9 pan means easy clean-up. Try fun and delicious S'mores Cobbler (page 274) or Healthy Oatmeal Apple Crisp (page 254) for desserts they are sure to love!

We are pleased to bring you this cookbook that is chock-full of fresh, fun and satisfying recipes that you can make in your hard-working 13x9-inch pan. Enjoy!

Sincerely,
Jo Ann & Vickie

About this Book

There are some items in our kitchen that we depend upon...and the 13x9 pan is one of them! Whether it is a dependable metal pan that you have had for years or a new colorful ceramic version that you want to try, you will love to showcase your cooking talents with family & friends using this tried & true pan.

In this book you will find dozens of recipes that all have one thing in common...they all are made in a 13x9 pan. You may think this favorite pan is only for casseroles, and in this book you'll find the best casseroles ever! But you'll also find appetizer ideas, sandwich recipes, pasta bakes and yummy desserts that you make in this extraordinary pan. One pan, yummy food, easy clean-up...what more could you want?

We know you will enjoy and treasure this fun-filled cookbook with fresh and delicious recipes that you can make for every meal of the day...and each and every recipe is made in your much-loved 13x9 pan!

Getting to Know Your Hard-Working 13x9 Pan

You probably have a favorite 13x9 pan...and cooking and baking in it is as easy as can be. Here a few tips about that favorite pan that might make your time in the kitchen even easier and more fun.

Sizes, Shapes and Materials

We usually think of a 13x9-inch baking pan as a metal rectangle pan. It can come in a variety of metal finishes. That same size pan can also be made in glass, cast iron or stoneware. These pans can be used interchangeably in recipes even though the dimensions can be slightly different depending on the manufacturer.

A 13x9-inch baking pan has a volume of 3 quarts and you can use it for any recipe that calls for a 3-quart casserole dish. The casserole dish can be oval, curved edge or basically rectangular.

A 13x9-inch baking pan is almost twice the size of an 8x8-inch baking pan. If you have a recipe that calls for an 8 x 8-inch pan, you can double the recipe and bake it in your 13x9 pan. The baking time will be longer. If you have a favorite sheet-pan recipe, you can use two 13x9-inch baking pans instead of one sheet pan when baking the recipe. A sheet pan will give more browning than a 13x9-inch pan, but baking time in the small pans will be a little less.

Metal 13x9-inch baking pans can be found in a variety of materials. Metal pans can be made from steel, aluminum, or metal with non-stick surfaces. Some have textures in the metal and some are smooth. Some are made out of natural aluminum substances. If it is labeled "organic aluminum," that signifies that this pan should last you a lifetime without rusting. It is powerful and durable. Aluminum has amazing heat conductivity so that helps with the cooking and even-baking of the dish. Metal pans are great to use for baking bars, cakes and brownies. Some come with metal or plastic lids for taking to potlucks or other events.

Glass 13x9-inch baking pans are nonreactive and work well for most any recipe. They are excellent for recipes that have acidic ingredients such as tomatoes, citrus or berries. They also work well for egg dishes.

Stoneware 13x9-inch baking pans are also non-reactive and can be used for most recipes. They come in a variety of colors and work well to serve the recipe right from the pan. A stoneware pan can usually be put under the broiler for finishing some dishes. Be sure and check the manufacturer's instructions on whether or not it is broiler safe.

Cast-Iron 13x9-inch baking pans are heavy-duty and work well for casseroles. They brown the edges nicely and hold the heat when serving.

Metal 13x9-inch baking pan

Glass 13x9-inch baking pan

Stoneware 13x9-inch baking pan

Cast-Iron 13x9-inch baking pan

Using the Right Pan

Whether you are baking a casserole or a pan of brownies, using the right pan is important for successful results. The recipe that you choose will call for a specific pan and that is because the volume of the batter or ingredients will fit into the pan and bake at the temperature and time suggested. If you do not have the suggested pan or want to change the pan, here are some helpful hints for using pans interchangeably.

Here's a handy chart in case you don't have the exact size pan or dish called for:

13"x9" baking pan = 3-quart casserole dish
9"x9" baking pan = 2-quart casserole dish
8"x8" baking pan = 1-1/2 quart casserole dish

Area of square/rectangle pans:

6 x 6 = 36 square inches
7 x 7 = 49 square inches
8 x 8 = 64 square inches
9 x 9 = 81 square inches
13 x 19 = 117 square inches
12 x 16 (half-sheet pan) = 192 square inches

Area of round pans:

5 inch = 20 square inches
6 inch = 29 square inches
7 inch = 39 square inches
8 inch = 50 square inches
9 inch = 64 square inches
10 inch = 79 square inches
12 inch = 113 square inches

Chapter One

Oven Lovin' Breakfasts & Breads

Begin your day just right with homemade goodies from the kitchen that you bake in one simple pan. If you love eggs (and who doesn't?) try Fluffy Baked Eggs or a Hearty Breakfast Casserole. If there is a sweet tooth in the family, whip up a Cinnamon Roll Casserole or an easy-to-make Baked Apple Pancake. Bread lovers will enjoy Southwestern Flatbread and Anytime Cheesy Herb Biscuits. Whatever you choose to make, your dish will be delicious and your clean-up will be done in a jiffy so you can get on with the great day ahead.

Felice Jones, Boise, ID

Breakfast Casserole

This is our go-to casserole for any family event. We usually make it for Sunday brunch but sometimes it becomes our main dish served with a fruit salad. It is good anytime!

Serves 8 to 10

32-oz. pkg. frozen diced
   potatoes
1 lb. bacon, diced and crisply
   cooked
1 onion, diced
1 green pepper, diced
1 ½ c. shredded Monterey Jack
   cheese
1 doz. eggs
1 c. milk
1 t. salt
1 t. pepper

Grease a 13"x9" baking pan. Layer ⅓ each of potatoes, bacon, onion, green pepper and cheese. Repeat the layers 2 more times, ending with a layer of cheese. In a large bowl, beat together eggs, milk, salt and pepper. Pour mixture over the layers in pan. Bake at 350 degrees for 45 minutes until eggs are set. Cut into squares and serve warm.

Breakfast Casserole

Connie Herek, *Bay City, MI*

Apple & Berry Breakfast Crisp

Use sliced strawberries instead of blueberries and it's just as tasty. Be sure to add a dollop of plain yogurt on top!

Makes 12 servings

6 apples, peeled, cored and thinly sliced
2 c. blueberries
3 T. brown sugar, packed
5 T. frozen orange juice concentrate, thawed
3 T. all-purpose flour
1½ t. cinnamon
Optional: vanilla yogurt

Combine all ingredients except yogurt in a large bowl; stir until fruit is evenly coated. Spoon into a lightly greased 13"x9" baking pan. Sprinkle Oat Topping evenly over fruit. Bake at 350 degrees for 30 to 35 minutes or until apples are tender. Serve warm with yogurt, if desired.

OAT TOPPING:

¾ c. quick-cooking oats, uncooked
5 T. brown sugar, packed
5 T. butter, melted
3 T. all-purpose flour

Combine all ingredients; mix well.

Jill Burton, *Gooseberry Patch*

Baked Eggs in Tomatoes

So pretty for a brunch...a delicious way to enjoy tomatoes from the farmers' market. I like to use fresh corn, but frozen works just fine as well.

Makes 6 servings

6 tomatoes, tops cut off
¼ t. pepper
½ c. corn, thawed if frozen
½ c. red pepper, diced
½ c. mushrooms, diced
2 T. cream cheese, softened and divided
6 eggs
2 t. fresh chives, minced
¼ c. grated Parmesan cheese

With a spoon, carefully scoop out each tomato, creating shells. Sprinkle pepper inside tomatoes. Divide corn, red pepper and mushrooms among tomatoes; top each with one teaspoon cream cheese. In a bowl, whisk together eggs and chives. Divide egg mixture among tomatoes; top with Parmesan cheese. Place filled tomatoes in a lightly greased 13"x9" baking pan. Bake, uncovered, at 350 degrees until egg mixture is set, about 45 to 50 minutes. Serve warm.

Baked Eggs in Tomatoes

Anne Muns, *Scottsdale, AZ*

Garden-Fresh Egg Casserole

This is a large recipe that is great for when the family gets together. Everyone loves it.

Serves 8 to 10

1 c. buttermilk
½ c. onion, grated
1 ½ c. shredded Monterey Jack cheese
1 c. cottage cheese
1 c. spinach, chopped
1 c. tomatoes, chopped
½ c. butter, melted
18 eggs, beaten

Mix all ingredients together; pour into a greased 13"x9" baking pan. Cover; refrigerate overnight. Bake at 350 degrees for 50 minutes to one hour.

Chip Woods, *Worthington, OH*

Chocolate Chip Oven Pancake

I made this for my boys when they were growing up. Now they make this for their own children!

Serves 4

3 eggs, beaten
½ c. milk
½ c. all-purpose flour
¼ t. salt
½ c. chocolate chips
1 T. butter, melted
Optional: chocolate chips, pancake syrup

In a bowl, whisk together eggs, milk, flour and salt until smooth. Stir in chocolate chips. Spread butter in a 13"x9" baking pan; add batter. Bake at 400 degrees for about 20 minutes, until cooked through. Serve topped with additional chocolate chips and pancake syrup if desired.

Chocolate Chip Oven Pancake

Eleanor Dionne, *Beverly, MA*

Apple & Walnut Scones

These scones are wonderful fresh from the oven with hot tea or coffee.

Makes 8 scones

2 ¼ c. all-purpose flour
½ c. sugar
2 t. baking powder
½ t. salt
½ c. butter
2 eggs, beaten
¼ c. milk
2 t. vanilla extract
1 t. lemon zest
1 c. cooking apple, peeled, cored and chopped
½ c. chopped walnuts
¼ c. light brown sugar, packed
1 t. cinnamon

In a large bowl, combine flour, sugar, baking powder and salt; mix well. Cut in butter with 2 knives until crumbly; set aside. In a small bowl, mix eggs, milk, vanilla and lemon zest. Stir into flour mixture; dough will be sticky. Stir in apple. Place dough into a greased 13"x9" baking pan and press into a 8-inch ball. In a small bowl, mix nuts, brown sugar and cinnamon; sprinkle over top. Flatten and cut dough into 8 wedges. Bake in a 350 degree oven for about 25 minutes or until golden.

Stuart Wilder, *Las Vegas, NV*

Bacon & Mushroom Baked Omelet

I like to use fresh mushrooms in my omelet without cooking them first, but feel free to sauté them first if you prefer.

Serves 4 to 6

8 eggs, beaten
½ lb. sliced mushrooms
¼ c. green onions, chopped
4 slices bacon, crisply cooked and crumbled
1 c. shredded Cheddar cheese
salt and pepper to taste

In a large bowl, mix together eggs, mushrooms, onion and bacon. Add salt and pepper to taste. Pour mixture into a greased 13"x9" baking pan. Sprinkle cheese over top. Bake, uncovered, at 350 degrees for 20 minutes, or until set.

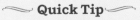

◦— Quick Tip —◦
Only using part of an onion? The remaining half will stay fresh for weeks when rubbed with butter or oil and stored in the refrigerator.

Bacon & Mushroom Baked Omelet

Jessica Kraus, *Delaware, OH*

Amish Breakfast Casserole

The blend of cheeses in this breakfast casserole makes it so delicious!

Makes 8 to 10 servings

1 lb. bacon, diced
1 sweet onion, chopped
1 green pepper, diced
10 eggs, beaten
1 ½ c. cream-style cottage cheese
4 c. frozen shredded hashbrowns, thawed
2 c. shredded Cheddar cheese
1 ½ c. shredded Monterey Jack cheese, divided

In a large skillet over medium heat, cook bacon, onion and green pepper until bacon is crisp; drain and set aside. In a large bowl, combine remaining ingredients, reserving ¼ cup of the Monterey Jack cheese. Stir bacon mixture into egg mixture. Transfer to a greased 13"x9" baking pan; sprinkle with reserved cheese. Bake, uncovered, at 350 degrees for 35 to 40 minutes, until set and bubbly. Let stand 10 minutes before cutting.

Hannah Hopkins, *Plainfield, VT*

Mother's Maple Spice Granola

I come from a family of six kids. This was one of my mother's yummy recipes that we had for breakfast or took to school. I still love it!

Serves 8

¾ c. maple syrup
½ c. butter, melted
1 t. vanilla extract
1 t. cinnamon
1 t. nutmeg
2 c. long-cooking oats, uncooked
1 ½ c. unsweetened flaked coconut
⅓ c. sesame seed
1 c. raisins
½ c. chopped walnuts

Mix maple syrup and butter thoroughly in a large bowl; add vanilla and spices. In a separate bowl, toss all the remaining ingredients together; stir into syrup mixture. Spoon into a greased 13"x9" baking pan. Bake at 350 degrees for 45 minutes, stirring every 15 minutes. Cool mixture before serving.

~ **Quick Tip** ~

Granola, a favorite breakfast treat, can be served so many ways. Serve it on top of yogurt or in a bowl with a little cream and fresh berries.

Mother's Maple Spice Granola

Angela Murphy, Tempe, AZ

Breakfast Stratas

These casseroles can be partially made ahead and assembled just before baking. Cook the sausage a day ahead and store in a plastic zipping bag in the refrigerator. The bread can also be cubed a day ahead and stored at room temperature in a plastic zipping bag. These casseroles can also be made in two 11"x7" baking pans.

Serves 20

2 1-lb. pkgs. hot ground pork
   sausage
16-oz. loaf sliced French bread,
   cut into 1-inch cubes
4 c. shredded Cheddar and
   Monterey Jack cheese blend,
   divided
8-oz. pkg. sliced mushrooms,
   coarsely chopped
4½-oz. can diced green chiles,
   drained
4-oz. can sliced ripe olives,
   drained
8 eggs, lightly beaten
4 c. milk
1 t. salt
1 t. onion powder
1 t. dry mustard
1 t. dried oregano
¼ t. pepper
Optional: sour cream, salsa

Cook sausage in a large skillet over medium-high heat, stirring until it crumbles and is no longer pink. Drain and set aside. Divide the bread cubes between a lightly greased 13"x9" baking pan and an 8"x8" baking pan. Divide 2 cups cheese over bread cubes. Sprinkle with cooked sausage, mushrooms, green chiles and olives. Whisk together eggs, milk and seasonings in a medium bowl. Pour mixture over casseroles. Sprinkle with remaining cheese. Bake, uncovered, at 350 degrees for one hour or until set. Garnish with sour cream and salsa, if desired.

~ Quick Tip ~

13"x9" baking pans come in a variety of colors and materials such as ceramic, cast iron, aluminum and more. Choose a colorful dish if you plan to serve the dish right from the pan.

Breakfast Stratas

Suzanne Vella, *Babylon, NY*

French Toast Berry Bake

This French toast can be made with a variety of spices. Choose the ones that your family loves and enjoy every bite!

Serves 12

12 slices French bread, sliced 1-inch thick
5 eggs, beaten
2½ c. milk
1¾ c. brown sugar, packed and divided
1½ t. vanilla extract
1¼ t. cinnamon
Optional: ½ t. nutmeg, ¼ t. ground cloves
Optional: 1 c. chopped pecans
½ c. butter, melted
2 c. blueberries, strawberries, raspberries and/or blackberries

Arrange bread slices in a greased 13"x9" baking pan; set aside. In a bowl, combine eggs, milk, one cup brown sugar, vanilla, cinnamon and desired spices. Whisk until blended; pour over bread. Cover and refrigerate for 8 hours to overnight. Let stand at room temperature 30 minutes before baking. Sprinkle with pecans, if using. Combine melted butter and remaining brown sugar; drizzle over top. Bake, uncovered, at 400 degrees for 30 minutes. Sprinkle with berries and bake an additional 10 minutes, or until a fork comes out clean.

Amy Butcher, *Columbus, GA*

Fluffy Baked Eggs

Who would have thought to combine pineapple and eggs? After you taste this yummy recipe, you'll see why it is our family favorite!

Makes 12 servings

14 eggs, beaten
3 slices bacon, crisply cooked and crumbled
1⅓ c. cottage cheese
8-oz. can crushed pineapple in own juice, drained
1 t. vanilla extract
Garnish: cooked bacon crumbles, chopped fresh parsley

In a large bowl, blend together eggs, bacon, cottage cheese, pineapple and vanilla; spoon into a greased 13"x9" baking pan. Bake, uncovered, at 350 degrees for 40 to 45 minutes or until center is set and a toothpick inserted in center comes out clean. Allow baking pan to stand 5 minutes before slicing. Garnish with cooked bacon crumbles and parsley if desired; cut into squares.

Fluffy Baked Eggs

Rita Morgan, *Pueblo, CO*

Scalloped Bacon & Eggs

This casserole will make a hit with all egg-lovers!

Serves 6 to 8

¼ c. onion, chopped
3 T. butter
3 T. all-purpose flour
2 c. milk
1 ½ c. shredded Cheddar cheese
½ t. dry mustard
9 eggs, hard-boiled, peeled and sliced
1 t. salt
¼ t. pepper
2 c. potato chips, crushed
12 slices bacon, crisply cooked and crumbled

In a skillet over medium heat, sauté onion in butter until translucent; stir in flour. Gradually add milk and cook, stirring constantly, until thickened. Add cheese and mustard, stirring until cheese melts. Place half the egg slices in a greased 13"x9" baking pan. Sprinkle with salt and pepper. Cover with half each of the cheese sauce, potato chips and bacon. Repeat layers. Bake, uncovered, at 350 degrees for 15 to 20 minutes.

Audra Vanhorn-Sorey, *Columbia, NC*

Pumpkin French Toast Bake

This recipe is delightful on a cool fall morning. Just pull it from the fridge and bake...the delicious aroma will bring everyone to the breakfast table!

Serves 10

1 loaf crusty French bread, cubed
7 eggs, beaten
2 c. milk
½ c. canned pumpkin
2 t. pumpkin pie spice, divided
1 t. vanilla extract
3-½ T. brown sugar, packed
Optional: ½ c. chopped pecans
Garnish: maple syrup

Spread bread cubes in a greased 3-quart casserole dish or a 13"x9" baking pan; set aside. In a large bowl, whisk together eggs, milk, pumpkin, 1½ teaspoons spice and vanilla. Pour evenly over bread; press down with spoon until bread is saturated. Cover and refrigerate overnight. In the morning, uncover and top with brown sugar, remaining spice and pecans, if desired. Bake, uncovered, at 350 degrees for 35 to 45 minutes, until golden. Serve with maple syrup.

Pumpkin French Toast Bake

Tracie Spencer, *Rogers, KY*

Hearty Breakfast Casserole

This will be a meat-eater's favorite breakfast casserole. Serve with some fresh fruit for a delicious way to start the day.

Serves 12

6 to 8 bread slices
3-oz. pkg. ready-to-use bacon crumbles
1 lb. cooked ham, diced, or ground pork
   sausage, browned
2 c. shredded Cheddar cheese
10 eggs, beaten
1 c. milk
1 t. salt
1 t. pepper

Arrange bread slices in a single layer in a greased 13"x9" baking pan; top with bacon and ham or sausage. Sprinkle with cheese. Whisk together remaining ingredients. Pour egg mixture over top. Cover with aluminum foil and refrigerate overnight. Bake, covered, at 350 degrees for 45 minutes to one hour, until center is set.

Amy Ott, *Greenfield, IN*

Cinnamon Roll Casserole

Ooey-gooey and irresistible! This recipe is great for special mornings...just brew the coffee, serve and enjoy!

Serves 6 to 8

2 12-oz. tubes refrigerated cinnamon rolls,
   separated
4 eggs
½ c. whipping cream
3 T. maple syrup
2 t. vanilla extract
1 t. cinnamon
¼ t. nutmeg

Cover the bottom of a greased 13"x9" baking pan with cinnamon rolls from one tube, adding one or 2 more rolls from remaining tube if necessary. Set aside icing packets. In a bowl, whisk together eggs, cream, maple syrup, vanilla and spices; drizzle over rolls. Break remaining rolls into bite-size chunks; place on top. Spoon one packet of icing over top; refrigerate remaining icing. Bake at 350 degrees for 30 minutes, or until rolls are set. Just before serving, drizzle with remaining icing.

Cinnamon Roll Casserole

Barb Rudyk, *Alberta, Canada*

Baked Apple Pancake

Mmm...tender apples, brown sugar and cinnamon. A sweet way to start the day!

Serves 6 to 8

4 apples, peeled, cored and sliced
½ c. butter, softened and divided
½ c. brown sugar, packed
1 t. cinnamon
6 eggs, beaten
1 c. all-purpose flour
1 c. milk
3 T. sugar

Combine apples, ¼ cup butter, brown sugar and cinnamon in a microwave-safe bowl. Microwave on high setting about 2 to 4 minutes, until tender. Stir; spoon into a lightly greased 13"x9" baking pan and set aside. In a separate bowl, combine remaining ingredients; whisk until smooth and spread over apple mixture. Bake, uncovered, at 425 degrees for 25 minutes. Cut into squares; serve warm.

Lori Hurley, *Fishers, IN*

French Toast Casserole

A really simple way to make French toast for a crowd. Pop it in the fridge the night before, then all you have to do is bake it the next day. Make for breakfast or serve with bacon for a great dinner!

Makes 6 to 8 servings

1 c. brown sugar, packed
½ c. butter
2 c. corn syrup
1 loaf French bread, sliced
5 eggs, beaten
1 ½ c. milk
Garnish: powdered sugar, maple syrup

Melt together brown sugar, butter and corn syrup in a saucepan over low heat; pour into a greased 13"x9" baking pan. Arrange bread slices over mixture and set aside. Whisk together eggs and milk; pour over bread, coating all slices. Cover and refrigerate overnight. Uncover and bake at 350 degrees for 30 minutes, or until lightly golden. Sprinkle with powdered sugar; serve with warm syrup.

French Toast Casserole

Rita Morgan, *Pueblo, CO*

Southwestern Flatbread

Yum...hot fresh-baked bread to enjoy for breakfast with a cup of fresh fruit! Easy to change up to Italian flavors too, with oregano and Parmesan cheese.

Makes about 15 pieces

2 t. olive oil, divided
11-oz. tube refrigerated crusty French loaf
½ c. roasted sunflower kernels
1 t. chili powder
½ to 1 t. coarse salt

Brush a 13"x9" baking pan with one teaspoon oil; unroll dough into pan. Push dough into the pan to fill, making a rectangle. Drizzle dough with remaining oil; brush over dough. In a small bowl, combine sunflower kernels and chili powder; mix well and sprinkle over the dough. Firmly press sunflower kernels into dough; sprinkle top with salt. Bake at 375 degrees for 12 to 16 minutes, until golden. Remove flatbread to a wire rack; cool 10 minutes. Tear or cut into pieces.

Lizzy Burnley, *Ankeny, IA*

Lizzy's Make-Ahead Egg Casserole

This recipe is a favorite for breakfast, lunch or dinner. And preparing it ahead makes it that much easier!

Serves 12

1 doz. eggs, beaten
1 c. cooked ham, diced
3 c. whole milk
12 frozen waffles
2 c. shredded Cheddar cheese

In a large bowl, beat eggs. Stir in ham and milk. Grease a 13"x9" baking pan. Place one layer of waffles in the bottom of the pan. Pour half of egg mixture over waffles. Sprinkle with half of the cheese. Continue layering waffles, egg mixture and cheese. Cover and refrigerate overnight. Uncover and bake at 350 degrees for about one hour or until eggs are set.

Lizzy's Make Ahead Egg Casserole

Sue Cherry, *Starkville, MS*

Rise & Shine Torte

*An easy meal that will impress your guests...
also try it with mushrooms and spinach.*

Makes 10 servings

10 eggs, beaten
⅓ c. milk
2 T. all-purpose flour
½ t. salt
½ c. shredded sharp Cheddar cheese
1 c. shredded Monterey Jack cheese
¼ c. jalapeño peppers, seeded and finely
   chopped

Combine eggs, milk, flour and salt in a large bowl;
mix well. Add remaining ingredients, mixing
well. Pour into a well-greased 13"x9" baking pan;
bake, uncovered, at 350 degrees for 35 minutes.
Cut into squares to serve.

Mary Ann Lewis, *Olive Branch, MS*

Best-Ever Breakfast Bars

*These chewy, nutty, healthy bars are great to
grab in the morning for a perfect take-along
breakfast.*

Makes one dozen

1½ c. oat-based granola
1½ c. quick-cooking oats, uncooked
¾ c. all-purpose flour
⅔ c. brown sugar, packed
¼ t. cinnamon
¾ c. unsalted mixed nuts, coarsely chopped
¾ c. dried fruit, chopped into small pieces
2 T. ground flaxseed meal
⅔ c. canola oil
½ c. honey
½ t. vanilla extract
1 egg, beaten

Combine granola and next 7 ingredients in
a large bowl. Whisk together oil, honey and
vanilla; stir into granola mixture. Add egg; stir
to blend. Press mixture into a parchment
paper-lined 13"x9" baking pan. Bake at
325 degrees for 30 to 35 minutes, until lightly
golden around the edges. Remove from oven
and cool 30 minutes to one hour. Slice into bars.

Best-Ever Breakfast Bars

Suzy McNeilly, *Colfax, WA*

Herby Bubble Bread

Perfect to take to a potluck or serve with soup. If you're looking for extra oomph, shake in some red pepper flakes!

Serves 6 to 8

3 1-lb. loaves frozen bread dough, thawed
   but still chilled
¼ c. olive oil
3 T. Italian salad dressing mix
1 c. shredded sharp Cheddar cheese
1 t. garlic, minced
1 red onion, finely chopped

Cut dough into one-inch cubes; place in a large bowl. Pour remaining ingredients over top. Using your hands, toss until dough cubes are coated. Transfer dough cubes to a greased 13"x9" baking pan. Place in a warm area; cover and let rise until double in size. Bake at 350 degrees for 20 to 25 minutes, until golden.

Natasha Morris, *Ulysses, KS*

Egg Casserole Deluxe

This recipe is so versatile. My youngest daughter made this for her sister's bridal shower...it was a big hit with the bride-to-be and the guests! For a quick weeknight dinner, just add a fruit salad and dinner is done.

Serves 8

2 T. butter
1 c. sliced mushrooms
18 eggs, beaten
8-oz. container sour cream
1 c. shredded Cheddar cheese
2.52-oz. pkg. pre-cooked bacon, crumbled and
   divided

Melt butter in a large skillet over medium heat. Sauté mushrooms and set aside. Add eggs; cook and stir until softly scrambled. Stir in sour cream, mushrooms, cheese and half of bacon. Transfer to a lightly greased 13"x9" baking pan. Sprinkle remaining bacon on top. Bake, uncovered, at 350 degrees for 30 minutes.

Egg Casserole Deluxe

Rita Morgan, *Pueblo, CO*

Herbed Cheese Focaccia

This savory bread is a favorite, scrumptious for snacking or to accompany a tossed salad.

Serves 12 to 14

13.8-oz. tube refrigerated pizza dough
1 onion, finely chopped
2 cloves garlic, minced
2 T. olive oil
1 t. dried basil
1 t. dried oregano
½ t. dried rosemary
1 c. shredded mozzarella cheese

Grease a 13"x9" baking pan. Open pizza dough and press into pan, pressing with fingers to form indentations; set aside. Sauté onion and garlic in oil in a skillet; remove from heat. Stir in herbs; spread mixture evenly over dough. Sprinkle with cheese. Bake at 400 degrees for 10 to 15 minutes, until golden.

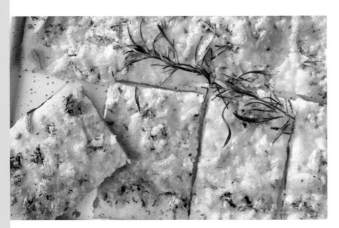

Connie Hilty, *Pearland, TX*

Breakfast Pizza

Is there anything better than pizza for breakfast? You are going to love this recipe!

Serves 2 to 4

11-oz. tube refrigerated thin-crust pizza dough
14-oz. can pizza sauce
16-oz. container ricotta cheese
¼ c. fresh oregano, chopped
favorite pizza toppings
4 eggs
salt and pepper to taste

Roll out dough into a 13-inch by 9-inch rectangle; transfer to a greased 13"x9" baking pan. Spread pizza sauce on dough, leaving a ½-inch border. Top with cheese, oregano and other pizza toppings. Bake at 500 degrees for 4 to 5 minutes, or until crust begins to turn golden. Crack each egg into a small bowl and slip onto pizza, being careful not to break the yolks. Bake for another 5 minutes, until eggs are done as desired.

Breakfast Pizza

Vickie, *Gooseberry Patch*

Jack-o'-Lantern Bread

Kids love these! Marinara sauce is great for dipping. Follow package directions for thawing bread dough. If making ahead, wrap cooled bread airtight and keep at room temperature up to one day or freeze to store longer. Reheat (thaw, if frozen), loosely covered with foil, in a 350-degree oven 10 to 15 minutes or until warm.

Serves 4 to 6

1-lb loaf frozen bread dough, thawed
1 T. egg, beaten
1 ½ t. milk

Place the loaf in a greased bowl. Cover bowl with plastic wrap and let rise until doubled, 45 minutes to one hour. Punch down dough ball. Transfer ball to a greased 13"x9" baking pan. With greased hands or a lightly floured rolling pin, flatten ball into a 8"x 9" oval. Cut out eyes, nose and mouth; openings should be at least 1½ to 2 inches wide. Cover the shaped dough lightly with plastic wrap and let rise until puffy, about 20 minutes. Mix egg with milk; brush over dough. Bake at 350 degrees for 20 to 25 minutes or until golden. Cool on a wire rack. Serve warm or cool.

Nick Jenner, *Chicago, IL*

Steak & Eggs

I make breakfast for my golf buddies sometimes before we hit the links. Cooking everything in one pan makes clean-up easy.

Serves 3 to 4

2 T. olive oil
1 ½ lbs. potatoes, peeled and diced
2 cloves garlic, minced
¼ c. grated Parmesan cheese
½ t. salt, divided
½ t. pepper, divided
1 lb. beef sirloin steak, sliced into
   1-inch pieces
3 to 4 eggs
Optional: chopped fresh chives

Spread oil in a 13"x9" baking pan. Spread potatoes over oil. Sprinkle with garlic and cheese; toss to combine. Sprinkle with half each of salt and pepper. Bake at 400 degrees for 20 to 25 minutes, until potatoes are golden. Remove pan from oven; preheat oven to broil. Season beef with remaining salt and pepper; add to pan in a single layer. With the back of a spoon, create 3 to 4 wells in potato mixture. Gently crack eggs into wells. Broil until egg whites have set and beef is cooked through. Garnish with chives, if desired.

Steak & Eggs

Carla Turner, *Salem, OR*

Make-Ahead French Toast

This wonderful make-ahead dish is perfect for brunches. With the prep time being the day before, I'm free to visit with friends & family.

Serves 15

3 T. butter
2 baking apples, peeled, cored and sliced
1/3 c. brown sugar, packed
1 T. dark corn syrup
1 t. cinnamon
8 slices French bread, 1-inch thick
3 eggs, beaten
1 c. milk
1 t. vanilla extract

Melt butter in a heavy skillet over medium heat. Reduce heat to medium-low; add apples and cook, stirring occasionally, until tender. Stir in brown sugar, corn syrup and cinnamon. Cook and stir until brown sugar dissolves. Pour apple mixture into a 13"x9" baking pan. Arrange bread slices in one layer on top of apple mixture; set aside. In a medium bowl, whisk together remaining ingredients; pour over bread slices. Cover with plastic wrap and refrigerate overnight. Remove plastic wrap and bake at 375 degrees for 30 to 35 minutes, or until firm and golden. Cool 5 minutes in pan, then invert onto a serving platter.

Naomi Cooper, *Delaware, OH*

Anytime Cheesy Herb Biscuits

So easy...you can whip them up in minutes! If you have fresh herbs in your garden, choose the ones you like.

Makes about 1 1/2 dozen

2 c. biscuit baking mix
2/3 c. milk
1/2 c. shredded Cheddar cheese
1 T. fresh parsley, chopped
1 T. fresh chives, chopped
1/4 c. butter, melted
1/4 t. garlic powder
Garnish: chopped fresh herbs

Mix together first 5 ingredients until a soft dough forms; beat vigorously for 30 seconds. Drop by rounded tablespoonfuls into a greased 13"x9" baking pan. Bake at 400 degrees for 8 to 10 minutes or until golden. Whisk together butter and garlic powder; spread over warm biscuits. Garnish with fresh herbs.

Anytime Cheesy Herb Biscuits

Dobie Hill, *Lubbock, TX*

Buttermilk Cinnamon Rolls

These no-yeast rolls are super easy and fast to make and are always a treat!

Serves 15

3 c. all-purpose flour
4 t. baking powder
¼ t. baking soda
1 t. salt
½ c. cold butter
1 ½ c. buttermilk
¼ c. butter, softened
½ c. sugar
1 t. cinnamon
Optional: dried cranberries,
    chopped nuts

In a large bowl, combine flour, baking powder, baking soda and salt; cut in cold butter until crumbs form. Stir in buttermilk until well blended; knead dough on a lightly floured surface for 4 to 5 minutes. Roll out to ¼-inch thickness; spread softened butter over dough to edges. In a small bowl, mix sugar and cinnamon; sprinkle over dough. Add cranberries and nuts if using. Roll up jelly-roll style; cut into ½-inch slices. Place in a greased 13"x9" baking pan. Bake at 400 degrees for 10 to 12 minutes.

Buttermilk Cinnamon Rolls

Pamela Delacruz, *Mount Vernon, WA*

Pamela's Garlic Bread

People will gather in the kitchen waiting for this to come out of the oven!

Makes 12 servings

8-oz. pkg. cream cheese, softened
4-oz. can chopped black olives, drained
4 green onions, chopped
2 to 3 cloves garlic, finely chopped
1 T. Italian seasoning
¼ c. butter, softened
1 loaf French bread, halved lengthwise

In a bowl, combine all ingredients except bread; mix until well blended. Evenly spread mixture over cut sides of bread. Place bread in an ungreased 13"x9" baking pan. Bake, uncovered, at 350 degrees for 10 to 15 minutes, until bubbly and golden. Cool slightly and slice.

Liz Plotnick-Snay, *Gooseberry Patch*

Artichoke-Parmesan Breakfast Casserole

I like to serve this with a green salad when I have friends over for brunch.

Serves 6 to 8

14-oz. can artichokes, drained and chopped
¾ c. shredded Cheddar cheese
¾ c. shredded Monterey Jack cheese
10 eggs
1 c. sour cream
⅓ c. grated Parmesan cheese
Garnish: salsa

Spread artichokes evenly over bottom of greased 13"x9" baking pan. Top with Cheddar and Monterey Jack cheeses; set aside. In a large bowl, whisk together eggs and sour cream. Pour over cheese. Top egg mixture with Parmesan cheese. Bake, uncovered, at 350 degrees for 30 to 35 minutes, until set. Garnish with salsa.

> ~ **Quick Tip** ~
> Chop fresh herbs and onions and keep in small plastic bags in the freezer to have handy for busy cooking days.

Artichoke-Parmesan Breakfast Casserole

Lynn Williams, *Muncie, IN*

Soft Sesame Bread Sticks

Delicious with just about any soup or salad!

Makes one dozen

1 ¼ c. all-purpose flour
2 t. sugar
1½ t. baking powder
½ t. salt
⅔ c. 2% milk
2 T. butter, melted
2 t. sesame seed

In a small bowl, combine flour, sugar, baking powder and salt. Gradually add milk; stir to form a soft dough. Turn dough onto a floured surface; knead gently 3 to 4 times. Roll into a 10-inch by 5-½ inch rectangle; cut into 12 bread sticks. Place butter in a 13"x9" baking pan; coat bread sticks in butter and sprinkle with sesame seed. Bake at 425 degrees for 14 to 18 minutes, until golden.

Nelda Columbo, *Port Arthur, TX*

Strawberry French Toast

We share this special breakfast when the grandchildren visit. Depending on the size of your bread loaf, you might need to use less milk.

Serves 4 to 8

1 uncut loaf French bread
8-oz. pkg. cream cheese, softened
10-oz. jar strawberry jam
6 eggs, beaten
2 c. milk
½ c. sugar
Optional: powdered sugar

Slice bread crossways in one-inch slices, without cutting through bottom crust. Slice once down the center lengthwise, again without cutting through bottom crust. Place loaf in a buttered 13"x9" baking pan. Spread cream cheese over top of loaf; spread jam over cheese and set aside. In a bowl, beat together eggs, milk and sugar; pour over loaf. Cover with aluminum foil and refrigerate overnight. Bake, covered, at 350 degrees for 45 minutes. Uncover and bake for 15 minutes more. Cut slices apart for serving; sprinkle with powdered sugar, if desired.

Strawberry French Toast

Tammy Walker, *Kansas City, MO*

Crescent Breakfast Casserole

Quick & easy for a chilly morning...it makes a hearty, filling supper too.

Serves 8

8-oz. tube refrigerated crescent rolls
6 to 8 eggs, beaten
¼ c. milk
¾ c. finely shredded Cheddar cheese
½ c. bacon, crisply cooked, or ground pork
  sausage, browned and crumbled
salt and pepper to taste

Line the bottom and sides of a lightly greased 13"x9" baking pan with unrolled crescents. Pinch seams together to seal; set aside. In a bowl, stir together remaining ingredients. Pour egg mixture over crescents in baking pan. Bake, uncovered, at 350 degrees for about 20 minutes, until golden and center is set.

Carol Field Dahlstrom, *Ankeny, IA*

Pesto Pepper Roll-Ups

These are so quick to make and are so yummy served with warm marinara sauce for dipping.

Serves 12

16-oz. loaf frozen bread dough, thawed
½ c. bottled basil pesto sauce
⅓ c. bottled roasted red sweet peppers,
  drained, patted dry, and chopped
½ c. shredded Parmesan cheese, divided

Coat a 13"x9" baking pan with non-stick vegetable spray. On a lightly floured surface, roll bread dough into a 13-inch by 9-inch rectangle. Spread pesto over dough to edges. Sprinkle roasted peppers and ⅓ cup cheese over pesto. Starting from a long side, roll up rectangle creating a spiral. Pinch dough to seal seams. Slice roll into 12 pieces. Arrange pieces in the prepared pan. Cover; let rolls rise in a warm place until nearly double in size, about 30 minutes. Uncover rolls and sprinkle with the remaining cheese. Bake at 375 degrees for 20 to 25 minutes, until golden. Immediately remove rolls from pan and serve warm.

Pesto Pepper Roll-Ups

Georgia Muth, *Penn Valley, CA*

Cranberry-Pecan Coffee Cake

These tender cranberry-and-nut streusel loaves are perfect to serve with coffee or tea.

Serves 8

½ c. butter, softened
1 c. sugar
2 eggs
2 c. all-purpose flour
2 t. baking powder
½ t. baking soda
½ t. salt
8-oz. container sour cream
1 t. almond extract
1 t. vanilla extract
16-oz. can whole-berry
   cranberry sauce
1 c. coarsely chopped pecans

In a large bowl, beat butter at medium speed with an electric mixer until creamy. Gradually add sugar, beating well. Add eggs, one at a time, beating until blended after each addition. In another bowl, combine flour, baking powder, baking soda and salt. Add flour mixture to butter mixture alternately with sour cream, beginning and ending with flour mixture. Stir in extracts. Spoon ½ cup batter into the bottom of a 13"x9" baking pan. Gently stir cranberry sauce; spoon ¼ of the sauce over batter and spread lightly to edges. Sprinkle 4 tablespoons pecans over cranberry sauce. Repeat layers using remaining batter, cranberry sauce and pecans. Bake at 350 degrees for 48 to 50 minutes, until a toothpick inserted in center comes out clean. Cool in pan completely. Drizzle Almond Cream Glaze over cooled cake.

ALMOND CREAM GLAZE
¾ c. powdered sugar
2 T. whipping cream
½ t. almond extract

In a small bowl, mix together all ingredients. Stir until smooth. Cover until ready to use.

Cranberry-Pecan Coffee Cake

Beth Kramer, *Port St. Lucie, FL*

Orange Coffee Rolls

Perfect for any special morning, these rolls are our family favorite.

Makes 2 dozen

1 env. active dry yeast
¼ c. warm water, 110 to 115
   degrees
1 c. sugar, divided
2 eggs, beaten
½ c. sour cream
¼ c. plus 2 T. butter, melted
1 t. salt
2 ¾ to 3 c. all-purpose flour
2 T. butter, melted and divided
1 c. flaked coconut, toasted and
   divided
2 T. orange zest

Combine yeast and warm water in a large bowl; let stand 5 minutes. Add ¼ cup sugar, eggs, sour cream, melted butter and salt; beat at medium speed with an electric mixer until blended. Gradually stir in enough flour to make a soft dough. Turn dough out onto a well-floured surface; knead until smooth and elastic, about 5 minutes. Place in a well greased bowl, turning to grease top. Cover and let rise in a warm place (85 degrees), free from drafts, 1½ hours or until double in bulk. Punch dough down and divide in half. Roll one portion of dough into a 12-inch circle; brush with one tablespoon melted butter. Combine remaining sugar, ¾ cup coconut and orange zest; sprinkle half of coconut mixture over dough. Cut into 12 wedges; roll up each wedge, beginning at wide end. Place in a greased 13"x9" baking pan, point-side down. Repeat with remaining dough, butter and coconut mixture. Cover and let rise in a warm place, free from drafts, 45 minutes or until double in bulk. Bake at 350 degrees for 25 to 30 minutes or until golden. (Cover with aluminum foil after 15 minutes to prevent excessive browning, if necessary.) Spoon warm Glaze over warm rolls; sprinkle with remaining coconut.

GLAZE:
¾ c. sugar
½ c. sour cream
¼ c. butter
2 t. orange juice

Combine all ingredients in a small saucepan; bring to a boil. Boil 3 minutes, stirring occasionally. Let cool slightly. Makes one cup.

Orange Coffee Polls

Sandy Bernards, *Valencia, CA*

Quiche-Me-Quick

This quiche is so easy to make. Add some chopped veggies if you like.

Serves 10 to 12

1/2 c. butter
1/2 c. all-purpose flour
6 eggs, beaten
1 c. milk
16-oz. pkg. Monterey Jack cheese, cubed
3-oz. pkg. cream cheese, softened
2 c. cottage cheese
1 t. baking powder
1 t. salt
1 t. sugar

Melt butter in a saucepan; add flour. Cook and stir until smooth; beat in the remaining ingredients. Stir until well blended; pour into a greased 13"x9" baking pan. Bake at 350 degrees for 45 minutes.

Micki Stephens, *Marion, OH*

Rise & Shine Breakfast Pizza

You will enjoy tasting the layers of all your breakfast favorites in this dish!

Serves 8 to 10

2-lb. pkg. frozen shredded hashbrowns
1 1/2 c. shredded Cheddar cheese, divided
7 eggs, beaten
1/2 c. milk
salt and pepper to taste
10 pork breakfast sausage patties, cooked

Prepare hashbrowns according to package directions. Place in ungreased 13"x9" baking pan. Top with 1/2 cup cheese; set aside. Whisk together eggs and milk in a microwave-safe bowl; microwave on high 3 minutes. Scramble eggs well with a whisk. Return to microwave and cook 3 more minutes; whisk well to scramble. Layer eggs on top of cheese; add salt and pepper to taste. Top with remaining cheese. Arrange sausage patties on top. Bake at 400 degrees for 10 minutes, or until cheese is melted. Cut into squares or wedges to serve.

Rise & Shine Breakfast Pizza

Vickie Wiseman, *Liberty Township, OH*

French Toast with Praline Sauce

I can remember making this delicious recipe with my great-grandmother. She taught me that whenever I am using cinnamon, I should add some nutmeg and cardamom to enhance the flavor. I believe this was actually her mother's recipe, from the late 1800s. Grandma always used fresh-baked bread, but any good bread will work.

Makes 12 servings

1 loaf bread, sliced 1-inch thick
6 eggs
½ c. whipping cream
1 T. brown sugar, packed
2 t. vanilla extract
1 t. cinnamon
½ t. nutmeg
¼ t. cardamom

Set out bread slices for one to 2 hours to dry. In a large bowl, combine remaining ingredients. Beat with an electric mixer on medium speed until smooth and brown sugar is dissolved. Pour one cup of mixture into a greased 13"x9" baking pan. Arrange bread slices on top; pour remaining egg mixture evenly over bread. Cover and refrigerate overnight. If desired, heat a greased cast-iron skillet or electric griddle. Add bread slices, a few at a time; cook until golden on both sides. (This step adds color to the toast but may be omitted.) Return bread slices to baking pan. Spoon Pecan Praline Syrup over top. Bake at 350 degrees until set and golden, about 30 minutes.

PECAN PRALINE SYRUP:
1 T. butter
¾ c. brown sugar, packed
½ c. pure maple syrup
¾ c. chopped pecans, toasted

Melt butter in a saucepan over medium heat. Add brown sugar and maple syrup; cook and stir until smooth. Bring mixture to a boil. Reduce heat to low and simmer for one minute, stirring constantly. Stir pecans into syrup.

French Toast with Praline Sauce

Chapter Two

Starters & Snacks

Whether you are throwing a party or just need a snack to tide you over until the next meal, these easy-to-make starters and snacks will become your favorites. Sweet Potato Chili Wedges are super easy to make and add color and flavor to your appetizer table. Everyone loves a good party dip. Try Cheesy Chile Artichoke Dip or 7-Layer Mexican Dip...you won't have any leftovers! Need a simple snack? Honey-Glazed Snack Mix is a yummy treat with a glass of milk or iced tea. These one-pan goodies are sure to become your go-to recipes.

Stephanie D'Esposito, *Ravena, NY*

Hot & Melty Taco Dip

Get the party started with this panful of sassy, cheesy goodness!

Makes 8 servings

16-oz. can refried beans
1 ½ oz. pkg. taco seasoning mix
16-oz. container sour cream
8-oz. pkg. cream cheese, softened
16-oz. jar salsa
8-oz. pkg. shredded sharp Cheddar cheese
Garnish: shredded lettuce, chopped tomatoes,
    sliced black olives, jalapeño peppers, green
    onions
scoop-type tortilla chips

In a bowl, combine refried beans with taco seasoning. Spread in the bottom of a lightly greased 13"x9" glass baking pan; set aside. In a separate bowl, blend sour cream and cream cheese; spread over bean layer. Spoon salsa over sour cream layer; sprinkle cheese on top. Bake, uncovered, at 350 degrees for about 25 minutes, until beans are warmed through and cheese is melted. Garnish with desired toppings. Serve with tortilla chips.

Edythe Schipull, *Goldfield, IA*

Mini Ham Balls

These little meatballs are full of flavor and disappear fast at any gathering.

Makes about 20 balls

1 lb. lean ground beef
½ lb. ground ham
½ lb. ground mild Italian sausage
2 eggs, beaten
1 ½ c. dry bread crumbs
1 t. mustard
¾ c. catsup
1 T. green onion, chopped
1 T. Worcestershire sauce
½ t. salt
½ t. pepper
Topping: 3 T. catsup mixed with 1 T. brown
    sugar
Garnish: chopped fresh parsley

Mix all ingredients, except topping and garnish, together thoroughly. Make into balls about the size of a small walnut. Place in an ungreased 13"x9" baking pan. Spread Topping mixture on top of meatballs. Bake at 350 degrees for 35 to 45 minutes until cooked through. Add toothpicks if desired for easy serving.

Mini Ham Balls

Kathryn Harris, *Valley Center, KS*

Sweet Potato Chili Wedges

I just love the sweet & savory flavor of chili powder on sweet potatoes. This is perfect as an appetizer or as a small-plate side. I have even served it at Thanksgiving, instead of the usual sweet potato casserole. It will become a favorite of yours too.

Makes 6 servings

1 ⅓ lbs. sweet potatoes, cut into
   1-inch wedges
1 T. olive oil
¼ t. salt
⅛ t. pepper
¼ c. orange juice
1 T. honey
1¾ t. chili powder, divided
½ c. reduced-fat sour cream
¼ c. fresh cilantro, snipped
1 t. dried oregano
¼ t. pepper
Optional: sour cream, salsa

Place sweet potato wedges in a large plastic zipping bag. Add olive oil, salt and pepper to bag; toss to coat. Arrange potato wedges in an ungreased 13"x9" baking pan. In a small bowl, combine orange juice, honey and 1½ teaspoons chili powder; set aside. Bake potatoes, uncovered, at 450 degrees for 25 to 30 minutes, until tender, shaking pan occasionally and brushing 3 times with orange juice mixture. In a separate small bowl, combine sour cream, cilantro and remaining chili powder. Transfer potato wedges to a serving bowl. Serve with sour cream mixture for dipping.

⟨ Quick Tip ⟩

Here's a handy chart in case you don't have the exact size pan or dish called for:

13"x9" baking pan = 3-quart casserole dish
9"x9" baking pan = 2-quart casserole dish
8"x8" baking pan = 1 ½ quart casserole dish

Sweet Potato Chili Wedges

Jo Ann, *Gooseberry Patch*

Baja Shrimp Tacos

These baked tacos are always a special treat with all the yummy ingredients inside each tasty little serving. Everyone loves them!

Makes 8

2 lbs. shrimp, peeled and cleaned
2 c. shredded Cheddar cheese
$1/2$ c. mayonnaise
$3/4$ c. salsa
$1/4$ t. ground cumin
$1/4$ t. cayenne pepper
$1/4$ t. pepper
8   6-inch flour tortillas
Garnish: plain Greek yogurt, chopped fresh
   parsley

Chop shrimp, discarding tails. Mix shrimp, cheese, mayonnaise, salsa, cumin and peppers; spread one to 2 tablespoons on one tortilla. Place in a 13"x9" baking pan. Repeat with remaining tortillas filling the pan. Bake at 350 degrees for 15 minutes. Garnish as desired. Serve immediately.

Lynnette Jones, *East Flat Rock, NC*

Mapley Appetizers

With colorful green pepper and red maraschino cherries, this is a wonderful appetizer. The recipe was passed down to me by my husband's aunt.

Serves 8 to 10

15 $1/4$ oz. can pineapple tidbits, drained and
   juice reserved
$1/2$ c. maple syrup
$1/2$ c. vinegar
$1/3$ c. water
4 t. cornstarch
14-oz. pkg. mini smoked sausages
$2/3$ c. green pepper, cut into 1-inch squares
$1/2$ c. maraschino cherries

In a saucepan, blend reserved pineapple juice, maple syrup, vinegar and water; stir in cornstarch. Bring to a boil, stirring constantly. Pour into a 13"x9" baking pan. Add pineapple and remaining ingredients; stir gently. Bake at 350 degrees for about 30 minutes until bubbly. Serve immediately.

Mapley Appetizers

Carmen Clever, *Ashland, OH*

Flaky Sausage Wraps

Use hot and spicy pork sausage if you want a little more kick to these wraps.

Makes 8 servings

6-oz. pkg. ground pork sausage
¼ c. onion, chopped
¼ c. green pepper, chopped
1 clove garlic, minced
¼ t. mustard
3-oz. pkg. cream cheese, softened
1 T. green onion, chopped
8-oz. tube refrigerated crescent rolls, separated

In a skillet over medium heat, brown sausage with onion, pepper and garlic; drain. Reduce heat; add mustard, cream cheese and green onion, stirring until cheese melts. Cool slightly; place in a food processor. Process until smooth; spread on crescent rolls. Roll up crescent-roll style; arrange on an ungreased 13"x9" baking pan. Bake at 350 degrees for 10 to 12 minutes.

Hollie Moots, *Marysville, OH*

Cheesy Chile Artichoke Dip

This has become a staple at our family get-togethers. It's so easy to prepare...and once you've tried it, you can't stop dipping!

Serves 10 to 12

14-oz. jar artichokes, drained and chopped
6 ½ oz. jar marinated artichokes, drained and chopped
4-oz. can diced green chiles
¼ c. mayonnaise
2 c. shredded Cheddar cheese
tortilla chips, snack crackers

Combine artichokes, chiles, mayonnaise and cheese in a bowl; mix well. Transfer to a greased 13"x9" baking pan. Bake, uncovered, at 350 degrees for 20 to 25 minutes, until bubbly and cheese is melted. Serve with tortilla chips and crackers.

Cheesy Chile Artichoke Dip

Holly Child, *Parker, CO*

Green Chile Chicken Dip

Easy to make and packed with zesty flavor... sure to become your next favorite dip!

Serves 10 to 12

12-oz. can chicken, drained
2 8-oz. pkgs. cream cheese, softened and cubed
2 10¾-oz. cans cream of chicken soup
2 4-oz. cans diced green chiles
4-oz. can diced jalapeño peppers
tortilla chips

In a lightly greased 13"x9" baking pan, combine all ingredients except tortilla chips. Do not drain chiles or peppers. Stir until well blended. Bake, uncovered, at 350 degrees for 20 to 25 minutes, until hot and bubbly. Serve warm with tortilla chips.

Carrie Helke, *Schofield, WI*

Deluxe Cocktail Sausages

The surprising combination of brown sugar, pecans and cocktail sausages is super yummy!

Makes 2 dozen

½ c. butter
3 T. brown sugar, packed
3 T. honey
½ c. chopped pecans
8-oz. tube refrigerated crescent rolls, separated
24 mini smoked cocktail sausages

Preheat oven to 400 degrees. As oven is warming, melt butter in oven in a 13"x9" glass baking pan. When butter is melted, add brown sugar, honey and pecans; stir to coat bottom of the pan. Slice each crescent roll triangle into thirds. Roll each smaller triangle around one sausage. Place on butter mixture, seam-side down. Bake, uncovered, at 400 degrees for 15 minutes, or until golden.

⮞ Quick Tip ⮜

Hot! Hot! If a dish turns out spicier than you expected, turn down the heat by stirring in one tablespoon each of sugar and lemon or lime juice.

Deluxe Cocktail Sausages

Cathy Siebrecht, *Des Moines, IA*

Spicy Garlic Almonds

If you like almonds, you'll love this recipe with garlic and a kick of red pepper.

Makes about 3 cups

2 T. low-sodium soy sauce
2 t. hot pepper sauce
2 cloves garlic, pressed
1 lb. blanched whole almonds
1 T. butter, melted
1 t. pepper
¼ t. red pepper flakes

Combine sauces and garlic in a medium bowl. Add almonds, stirring until well coated. Brush butter in a 13"x9" baking pan. Spread almonds in pan. Bake at 350 degrees for 10 minutes. Sprinkle salt and peppers over almonds; return to oven for 15 minutes. Remove from oven; cool on pan. Store in an airtight container.

Renee Purdy, *Mount Vernon, OH*

7-Layer Mexican Dip

This colorful and tasty dish is one of our favorites. So quick to make and it goes fast!

Serves 12

2 16-oz. cans refried beans
1 c. salsa
16-oz. container sour cream
2 avocados, pitted, peeled and mashed
2 t. lime juice
3 cloves garlic, minced
2 c. shredded Cheddar cheese
4 green onions, diced
¼ c. black olives, sliced
1 ¼ c. diced tomatoes
1 T. fresh cilantro, chopped
tortilla chips

In a bowl, combine beans and salsa. Spread mixture in the bottom of a 13"x9" baking pan. Spread sour cream over beans. Mix avocados, lemon juice and garlic; layer over sour cream mixture. Sprinkle with cheese; top with onions, olives, tomatoes and cilantro. Chill before serving. Serve with tortilla chips.

7-Layer Mexican Dip

Roger Dahlstrom, *Ankeny, IA*

Bacon Wrapped Asparagus

This quick & easy appetizer takes only a few minutes to make and is always a favorite.

Serves 8

16 spears fresh asparagus, ends trimmed
8 slices of bacon
1/2 t. pepper

Wrap each asparagus spear with a half-slice of bacon. Arrange in a 13"x9" baking pan and sprinkle with pepper. Bake at 425 degrees until bacon is crisp, about 10 minutes. Serve immediately.

Judy Bailey, *Des Moines, IA*

Loaded Tater Tots

Everyone loves tater tots and adding some cheese and bacon only makes them better. Try this version of the popular starter for your next party.

Serves 8

28-oz. pkg. frozen tater tots
8-oz. pkg. shredded Cheddar cheese
2 T. butter,
1 T. chives, snipped
1 T. parsley, snipped
1 T. cilantro, snipped
2 T. flour
1 ½ c. milk
Garnish: crisp bacon, chopped fresh chives

Place tater tots on a baking sheet. Bake at 425 degrees for about 20 minutes, until crisp. Meanwhile, while the tater tots are baking, mix together cheese, butter, herbs, flour and milk in a saucepan. Cook until thick, about 10 minutes. Remove tater tots from baking sheet and place in a 13"x9" baking pan. Pour sauce on top and bake at 350 degrees for 15 minutes. Garnish as desired; serve immediately.

Loaded Tater Tots

Victoria Francis, *McHenry, IL*

Buffalo Potato Wedges

Wonderful as either an appetizer or a side dish.

Makes 6 to 8 servings

6 to 8 potatoes, sliced into wedges
1 to 2 T. olive oil
salt, pepper and garlic powder to taste
¼ c. butter, melted
½ c. hot pepper sauce
Optional: blue cheese salad dressing

Arrange potato wedges in a 13"x9" baking pan coated with non-stick vegetable spray. Drizzle with olive oil; sprinkle with seasonings. Bake at 375 degrees for about 30 minutes, until tender, tossing occasionally. Remove pan from oven. Combine butter and hot sauce in a microwave-safe cup. Microwave on high until butter is melted; stir to combine. Drizzle butter mixture over potato wedges; bake for an additional 15 minutes. Serve potato wedges with salad dressing for dipping, if desired.

Jane Kirsch, *Weymouth, MA*

Feta Squares

These tasty little goodies are so easy to make and go fast!

Makes 2 dozen

8-oz container crumbled feta cheese
8-oz. pkg. cream cheese, softened
2 T. olive oil
3 cloves garlic, finely chopped
1 loaf sliced party pumpernickel bread
1 pt. grape tomatoes, halved
2 to 3 T. fresh chives, finely chopped

In a bowl, mix feta cheese, cream cheese, olive oil and garlic. Spread mixture on pumpernickel bread slices. Place in 2 greased 13"x9" baking pans. Top each square with a tomato half; sprinkle with chives. Bake at 350 degrees for 15 minutes.

Feta Squares

Jordan Ray, *Clermont, FL*

Asian Chicken Wings

The cilantro in this recipe makes it one of my favorites.

Makes 2¹/₂ to 3 dozen

3 lbs. chicken wings, separated
2 T. olive oil
¹/₂ t. salt
2 t. pepper, divided
¹/₄ c. honey
1 T. low-sodium soy sauce
1 t. Worcestershire sauce
juice of 1 lime
zest of 2 limes
1 clove garlic, finely minced
1 T. fresh cilantro, chopped
1 t. red pepper flakes

Place wings in a greased 13"x9" baking pan. Drizzle wings with oil and toss to coat; sprinkle with salt and one teaspoon pepper. Bake at 400 degrees for 50 minutes; do not turn. Remove from oven. Using tongs, carefully lift wings from foil. Stir together remaining pepper and other ingredients. Drizzle ¹/₃ cup of sauce mixture over hot wings and toss to coat. Serve remainder of sauce separately for dipping.

Jan Temeyer, *Ankeny, IA*

Baby Potato Bites

These little bits of roasted goodness are a must for a quick appetizer.

Serves 4 to 6

¹/₄ c. olive oil
about 40 mini varied-color potatoes
¹/₄ c. grated Parmesan cheese
³/₄ t. salt
¹/₈ t. pepper
2 T. fresh parsley, chopped
2 T. fresh dill, chopped

Place oil and potatoes in a plastic zipping bag and shake to coat. Place remaining ingredients in another bag and shake to mix. Place oil-coated potatoes into herb mixture bag and shake to coat. Pour and arrange in a 13"x9" baking pan. Bake, uncovered, at 400 degrees for 45 minutes. Serve immediately.

Baby Potato Bites

Cindy Snyder, *Kittanning, PA*

Cheddar Apple Pie Dip

This is a great appetizer for a fall gathering of friends around a toasty fire. I also like to serve it at family gatherings. I serve it with whole-grain crackers or small pieces of toasted whole-grain bread.

Makes 8 servings

¼ c. brown sugar, packed
¼ t. cinnamon
1 red apple, cored and finely chopped
1 Granny Smith apple, cored and finely
   chopped
½ c. pecan pieces, coarsely chopped
8-oz. pkg. cream cheese, softened
1½ c. shredded sharp Cheddar cheese
¼ c. light sour cream

Combine brown sugar and cinnamon in a bowl; stir in apples and pecans. In a separate bowl, mix cream cheese and Cheddar cheese; add sour cream, stirring well to blend. Spread mixture in a 13"x9" baking pan. Top with apple mixture. Bake, uncovered, at 375 degrees for 20 minutes, or until heated through.

Diane Stevenson, *Marion, IA*

Yummy Snack Mix

A wonderful blend of flavors and textures makes this snack mix a great addition to any party.

Serves 20

2 c. bite-size crispy corn cereal
2 c. bite-size crispy rice cereal
2 c. round corn cereal
½ c. whole cashews
½ c. whole almonds
½ c. raisins
½ c. dried apricots, chopped
½ c. butter, melted
½ c. sugar
1 t. cinnamon

In a large bowl, combine cereals, cashews, almonds, raisins and apricots. Pour melted butter over mixture and toss lightly. In a separate bowl, mix together sugar and cinnamon; sprinkle over cereal mixture. Mix well. Pour into a 13"x9" baking pan. Bake at 250 degrees for one hour, stirring every 15 minutes. Cool. Store in airtight container.

Yummy Snack Mix

Jean Cerutti, *Kittanning, PA*

Oh-So-Hot Banana Peppers

Get ready for some spicy goodness!

Makes 18 servings

18 hot banana peppers
1 lb. ground turkey, browned and drained
1 c. whole-grain bread cubes, toasted
6-oz. pkg. pork-flavored stuffing mix, cooked
1 onion, chopped
1 zucchini, chopped
2 eggs, beaten
2 T. brown sugar, packed
½ c. shredded reduced-fat Cheddar cheese

Slice peppers lengthwise down one side to open up; rinse under running water, removing seeds. Combine turkey, dry bread cubes and cooked stuffing in a large bowl; add onion and zucchini. Stir in eggs and brown sugar; mix well. Spoon into peppers; arrange peppers in a lightly greased 13"x9" baking pan. Bake, uncovered, at 350 degrees for 1½ hours. Sprinkle with cheese; bake 10 more minutes, or until cheese is melted.

Darcy Geiger, *Columbia City, IN*

South-of-the-Border Dip

I make this dip for get-togethers...it's very easy and yummy!

Serves 8 to 10

2 lbs. ground pork sausage, browned and drained
2 10-oz. cans diced tomatoes with green chiles
1 c. favorite salsa
1 c. canned black beans, drained
1 c. canned corn, drained
16-oz. pkg. sharp Cheddar or queso blanco pasteurized process cheese, cubed
8-oz. pkg. cream cheese, cubed
tortilla chips

Combine sausage, tomatoes with juice and remaining ingredients except tortilla chips in a 13"x9" baking pan. Cover with aluminum foil and bake for about 30 minutes until cheese is melted. Serve warm with tortilla chips.

South-of-the-Border Dip

Lisa Sett, Thousand Oaks, CA

Jalapeño Popper Dip

Great for parties and watching football games! You'll want to wear a pair of disposable latex gloves when handling the peppers. If you like to make things a bit spicier, add a few drops of your favorite hot sauce.

Serves 10 to 12

6 to 8 slices bacon, crisply
  cooked and crumbled
2 8-oz. pkgs. cream cheese,
  softened
1 c. shredded Cheddar cheese
½ c. shredded mozzarella
  cheese
1 c. mayonnaise
4 to 6 jalapeño peppers, seeded
  and chopped
¼ c. green onions, diced
1 c. round buttery crackers,
  crushed
½ c. grated Parmesan cheese
¼ c. butter, melted

In a large bowl, combine all ingredients except crackers, Parmesan cheese and butter. Mix well; transfer to a buttered 13"x9" baking pan or 3-quart casserole dish. Combine remaining ingredients in a separate bowl; sprinkle over the top. Bake, uncovered, at 350 degrees for about 20 to 30 minutes, until hot and bubbly.

> ### ～ Quick Tip ～
> To prepare crispy bacon easily, try baking it in the oven! Place bacon slices on a broiler pan, place the pan in a cool oven and turn the temperature to 400 degrees. Bake for 12 to 15 minutes, turn bacon over and bake for another 8 to 10 minutes.

Jalapeño Popper Dip

Jen Thomas, *Santa Rosa, CA*

Game-Time Party Mix

Mix up a batch of this salty-sweet snack for guests to munch on...they'll love it!

Makes about 6 cups

2 c. bite-size crispy corn & rice cereal squares
2 c. mini pretzels
1 c. peanuts
1 c. caramels, unwrapped and coarsely chopped
11-oz. pkg. butterscotch chips

Combine cereal, pretzels, peanuts and caramels in a large bowl. In a microwave-safe bowl, microwave butterscotch chips on medium power for one minute; stir. Microwave an additional 15 seconds and stir; repeat until melted and smooth. Pour over cereal mixture; stir to coat evenly. Spread mixture into a 13"x9" baking pan coated with non-stick vegetable spray. Let stand 20 minutes, or until firm. Break into small pieces. Store in a loosely covered container.

Melissa Bordenkircher, *Lake Worth, FL*

Chinese Spareribs

Serve these at your next party and watch them disappear.

Serves 15

4 lbs. lean pork spareribs, sliced into serving-size portions
¼ c. hoisin sauce
¼ c. water
3 T. dry sherry
2 T. honey
1 T. low-sodium soy sauce
1 cloves garlic, minced

Place ribs in a very large plastic zipping bag. Mix remaining ingredients in a small bowl; pour over ribs. Seal bag; turn gently to coat ribs with marinade. Refrigerate for 6 hours to overnight, turning bag several times. Drain; reserve and refrigerate marinade. Place ribs in a 13"x9" baking pan. Cover with aluminum foil. Bake at 350 degrees for 1½ hours. Uncover; brush reserved marinade over ribs, discarding any remaining marinade. Bake, uncovered, an additional 30 minutes, or until tender.

Chinese Spareribs

Tara Horton, *Lewis Center, OH*

Cincinnati-Style Chili Dip

In Cincinnati, it's just not a tailgate party unless this warm dip is being passed around. Try to find a chili with cinnamon for an authentic Queen City experience!

Makes 10 servings

2 8-oz. pkgs. cream cheese, softened
2 10½-oz. cans Cincinnati-style or plain chili without beans
16-oz. pkg. shredded mild Cheddar cheese
tortilla chips

Spread cream cheese in an ungreased 13"x9" glass baking pan. Pour chili over top and sprinkle with cheese. Bake, uncovered, at 350 degrees for 15 to 20 minutes, until cheese is melted. Serve with tortilla chips.

Lori Ritchey, *Denver, PA*

Pepperoni Squares

Company coming and you need a quick appetizer? This will give your guests a warm welcome!

Serves 8 to 10

2 c. milk
2 eggs, beaten
1 ½ c. all-purpose flour
1 lb. Muenster cheese, diced
8-oz. pkg. pepperoni, chopped
½ t. dried oregano
¼ t. dried parsley
¼ t. pepper
1 c. shredded pizza-blend cheese
Garnish: warmed pizza sauce

Combine milk, eggs, flour, Muenster cheese, pepperoni and spices in a large bowl. Mix well; pour into a lightly greased 13"x9" baking pan. Bake at 350 degrees for 25 minutes. Remove from oven; sprinkle with pizza-blend cheese. Bake for an additional 5 to 8 minutes, until melted. Cool slightly; cut into squares. Serve with pizza sauce for dipping.

Pepperoni Squares

Cindy Elliott, *Modesto, IL*

Honey-Glazed Snack Mix

A perfect snack to munch while doing homework! This recipe is from my friend, Mary Beth Mitchell. I like the taste of this best when I use fresh honey from the farmers' market or orchard.

Makes about 10 cups

5 c. corn and rice cereal
3 c. mini pretzel twists
2 c. pecan halves
½ c. honey
½ c. butter, melted

Combine cereal, pretzels and pecans in a large bowl; set aside. Blend together honey and butter. Pour over cereal mixture; toss to coat. Pour into two 13"x9" baking pans. Bake at 300 degrees for 10 minutes. Stir and continue to bake an additional 10 to 15 minutes. Pour onto wax paper and cool completely. Store in airtight containers.

Judy Bailey, *Des Moines, IA*

Almond-Filled Dates

These are a sweet treat that serves as a dessert as well as an appetizer. The almond and cheese along with the fresh thyme add layers of flavor.

Serves 12

12 large medjool dates
6 slices bacon
½ c. toasted slivered almonds
½ c. grated Parmesan cheese
3 T. honey
1 t. fresh thyme, snipped

In a large skillet, cook bacon over medium heat until crisp. Transfer bacon to paper towels to drain; crumble bacon. In a bowl, stir together the bacon, almonds, and cheese. Make a slit down one side of each date and remove the pit. Spoon one tablespoon bacon mixture into each date; press date to shape around filling. Arrange dates, filling sides up, in an ungreased 13"x9" baking pan. Bake at 350 degrees for 12 to 15 minutes or until heated through and cheese is golden; cool slightly. Before serving, drizzle warm dates with honey and sprinkle with thyme.

Almond-Filled Dates

Lynn Williams, *Muncie, IN*

Pork & Apple Bites

We love party meatballs, but I was looking for something a little different. These are perfect for a fall tailgating party!

Makes about 3 dozen

1 lb. ground pork
¼ t. cinnamon
1 t. salt
⅛ t. pepper
½ c. Granny Smith apple, peeled, cored and grated
¼ c. soft rye bread crumbs
¼ c. chopped walnuts
½ c. water
½ c. apple jelly

In a large bowl; combine pork and seasonings; mix well. Add apple, bread crumbs and walnuts; mix gently until well blended. Form mixture into balls by tablespoonfuls. Working in batches, brown meatballs in a large skillet over medium heat. Drain, reserving drippings in skillet. Transfer meatballs to a 13"x9" baking pan. Cover and bake at 400 degrees for 20 minutes. Remove meatballs to a serving bowl; cover and set aside. Stir apple jelly into drippings in skillet; cook and stir until jelly is melted. Spoon sauce over meatballs.

Barb Bargdill, *Gooseberry Patch*

Cheesy Tuna Triangles

It's the sweet raisin bread and chopped apple that make these sandwiches stand out from all the rest.

Makes 8 servings

1 T. oil
¾ c. apple, cored and chopped
1 T. onion, chopped
7-oz. can albacore tuna, drained
¼ c. chopped walnuts
⅓ c. mayonnaise
2 t. lemon juice
⅛ t. salt
⅛ t. pepper
4 slices raisin bread, toasted and halved diagonally
4 slices cheese, halved diagonally

Heat oil in a skillet over medium heat; add apple and onion. Cook, stirring occasionally, about 5 minutes until tender. Remove from heat; transfer to a bowl. Stir in tuna, walnuts, mayonnaise, lemon juice, salt and pepper. Place toast slices in a 13"x9" baking pan. Top with tuna mixture and a slice of cheese. Bake at 425 degrees for about 10 minutes, or until cheese begins to melt.

Cheesy Tuna Triangles

Jen Sell, *Farmington, MN*

Seasoned Oyster Crackers

These are so good by themselves or sprinkled into homemade soups and stews. If you like a more buttery flavor, substitute butter for the oil.

Makes 24 servings

1 c. oil
2 1-oz. pkgs. ranch salad dressing mix
1 T. lemon pepper
1 T. dill weed
2 10-oz. pkgs. oyster crackers

Whisk first 4 ingredients together; pour over oyster crackers. Toss gently; spread in an 13"x9" baking pan. Bake at 225 degrees for one hour, stirring every 15 minutes. Cool and store in an airtight container.

Irene Robinson, *Cincinnati, OH*

Harvest Moon Popcorn

This is a great snack to have on hand instead of cereal mix. It's also terrific for lunchboxes.

Makes about 10 cups

8 c. popped popcorn
2 c. canned shoestring potatoes
½ c. butter, melted
1 t. Worcestershire sauce
1 t. lemon pepper seasoning
1 t. dried dill weed
½ t. onion powder
½ t. garlic powder
¼ t. salt

Combine popcorn and potatoes in a large bowl; set aside. In a separate small bowl, stir together remaining ingredients. Drizzle butter mixture over popcorn mixture; toss to coat. Pour into two 13"x9" baking pans. Bake, uncovered, at 350 degrees for 8 to 10 minutes. Cool; store in an airtight container.

Harvest Moon Popcorn

Chapter Three

Pasta Bakes

Move over ho-hum casseroles, these pasta bakes are sure to please! If you like classic macaroni, you'll love Aunt Judy's Baked Macaroni & Cheese...delicious! If you are a lasagna lover, you'll have to try Susan's Vegetable Lasagna or Chicken Lasagna with Roasted Red Pepper Sauce. You won't be disappointed! Penne pasta steals the show in our yummy Penne Sausage Bake and pasta shells take center stage in Taco-Filled Pasta Shells. Go ahead, grab the noodles and create these tasty pasta bakes.

Robin Kessler, *Fresno, CA*

Oodles of Noodles Chili Bake

Create a different dish by adding your favorite vegetables. It's foolproof and delicious either way!

Makes 4 servings

12-oz. pkg. wide egg noodles, uncooked
1 lb. ground beef
14 ½-oz. can diced tomatoes
15-oz. can corn, drained
15-oz. can chili
1 c. shredded Cheddar cheese, divided

Cook noodles according to package directions; drain and set aside. Meanwhile, brown beef in a skillet over medium heat; drain. Combine tomatoes with juice and remaining ingredients except ¼ cup cheese in a lightly greased 13"x9" baking pan. Top with remaining cheese. Bake, uncovered, at 350 degrees for about 20 minutes, or until heated through.

Lisanne Miller, *Wells, ME*

3-Cheese Pasta Bake

This yummy mac & cheese dish gets a great update with penne pasta and a trio of cheeses.

Serves 4

8-oz. pkg. penne pasta, uncooked
2 T. butter
2 T. all-purpose flour
1½ c. milk
½ c. half-and-half
1 c. shredded white Cheddar cheese
¼ c. grated Parmesan cheese
2 c. shredded Gruyère cheese, divided
1 t. salt
¼ t. pepper
⅛ t. nutmeg

Prepare pasta according to package directions; drain. Meanwhile, melt butter in a saucepan over medium heat. Whisk in flour until smooth; cook, whisking constantly, one minute. Gradually whisk in milk and half-and-half; cook, whisking constantly, 3 to 5 minutes or until thickened. Stir in Cheddar cheese, Parmesan cheese, one cup Gruyère cheese and seasonings until smooth. Stir together pasta and cheese mixture; pour into a lightly greased 13"x9" baking pan. Top with remaining Gruyère cheese. Bake, uncovered, at 350 degrees for about 15 minutes or until golden and bubbly.

3-Cheese Pasta Bake

Bec Popovich, *Columbus, OH*

Beefy Spinach Casserole

This pasta casserole is our go-to meal for every Thursday night. Everyone looks forward to it!

Serves 8

1 lb. ground beef
10-oz. pkg. frozen chopped spinach, thawed
    and drained
1 clove garlic, minced
salt and pepper to taste
16-oz. pkg. wide egg noodles, uncooked
10 ¾-oz. can cream of mushroom soup
2 ½ c. milk
1 c. American cheese, shredded

Brown beef in a skillet over medium heat; drain. Add spinach, garlic, salt and pepper; cook until heated through. Stir in egg noodles; spoon into a greased 13"x9" baking pan and set aside. Combine soup and milk; mix well to blend and stir gently into beef mixture. Sprinkle with cheese. Bake at 325 degrees for 45 minutes, until bubbly.

Bev Bornheimer, *Lyons, NY*

Penne Sausage Bake

The sausage and red pepper flakes make for a pasta bake that is full of flavor.

Serves 6

12-oz. pkg. penne pasta, uncooked
½ t. pepper
1 lb. hot or mild ground Italian pork sausage
3 cloves garlic, chopped
24-oz. jar marinara sauce with cabernet
    and herbs
½ t. red pepper flakes
½ t. salt
1 c. shredded mozzarella cheese
**Garnish: grated Parmesan cheese, chopped
    fresh parsley**

Cook pasta according to package directions. Meanwhile, cook sausage in a skillet over medium heat until browned; drain. Return sausage to pan. Add garlic and cook until tender, about 2 minutes. Stir in sauce and seasonings. Stir sauce mixture into cooked pasta; pour mixture into a greased 13"x9" baking pan. Top with mozzarella cheese. Bake, covered, at 375 degrees for 25 to 30 minutes, until bubbly and cheese has melted. Remove from oven; sprinkle with Parmesan cheese and parsley.

Penne Sausage Bake

Lori Joy, *Texico, IL*

Cheesy Zucchini & Beef Casserole

The zucchini is a great contrast to all the cheese in this rich dish.

Makes 6 to 8 servings

1 lb. ground beef
1 lb. ground pork sausage
2 c. zucchini, diced
1 c. onion, diced
1 c. green pepper, diced
1 c. tomato, diced
1 c. water
½ c. shell macaroni, uncooked
2 to 3 t. dried oregano
2 t. salt
1 ½ c. shredded Cheddar cheese
2 c. shredded mozzarella cheese

Brown beef and sausage well in a skillet over medium heat; drain. Add vegetables, water, uncooked macaroni, oregano and salt. Bring to a boil, stirring often. Reduce heat to low. Simmer for 25 minutes, or until vegetables and macaroni are tender and liquid is almost absorbed. Stir occasionally, adding a little more water if too dry. Remove from heat; cover and let stand 10 to 15 minutes. Stir in Cheddar cheese. Spoon into a greased 13"x9" baking pan; sprinkle with mozzarella cheese. Bake, uncovered, at 375 degrees until golden and cheese is melted, 5 to 10 minutes.

Michele Molen, *Mendon, UT*

Simple Baked Mostaccioli

My Italian grandmother always used this quick & easy recipe when she needed a dish for last-minute company or to send to a sick friend.

Serves 5

16-oz. pkg. mostaccioli pasta, uncooked
1 lb. ground beef
salt and pepper to taste
16-oz. jar pasta sauce, divided
8-oz. pkg. shredded mozzarella cheese, divided

Cook pasta according to package directions; drain. Meanwhile, brown beef in a skillet over medium heat. Drain; season with salt and pepper. Ladle a spoonful of pasta sauce into a greased 3-quart casserole dish or 13"x9" baking pan. Add half of cooked pasta. Layer with all of beef mixture, half of remaining sauce and half of cheese; repeat layers with remaining pasta, sauce and cheese. Bake, uncovered, at 375 degrees for about 20 minutes, until hot and bubbly.

Simple Baked Mostaccioli

Susan Province, *Strawberry Plains, TN*

Susan's Vegetable Lasagna

I created this recipe for my family as a way to add more vegetables to our meals. It's really versatile...use any fresh veggies you like.

Serves 8

2 t. olive oil
6 c. vegetables, diced, such as
    zucchini, yellow squash,
    carrots, broccoli, red pepper,
    mushrooms
1 onion, diced
2 cloves garlic, minced
2 T. low-sodium soy sauce
¼ t. pepper
½ t. dried basil
½ t. dried oregano
26-oz. jar marinara sauce,
    divided
9-oz. pkg. no-boil lasagna
    noodles, uncooked and
    divided
1 c. ricotta cheese
1 c. grated Parmesan cheese
1 c. shredded mozzarella cheese
1 t. dried oregano
¼ t. pepper
Optional: sour cream, salsa

Over medium-high heat, drizzle oil into a skillet. Add vegetables and onion; stir-fry until onion turns translucent. Add garlic and soy sauce; continue cooking until vegetables are tender. Season with pepper, basil and oregano. Spoon ½ cup sauce into an ungreased 13"x9" baking pan. Arrange ⅓ of the noodles on the bottom; spoon on half the ricotta cheese and half the Parmesan cheese. Top with half of the vegetables. Repeat again, ending with remaining noodles. Pour on the remaining sauce and sprinkle with mozzarella cheese. Bake, uncovered, at 350 degrees for 25 to 30 minutes.

Susan's Vegetable Lasagna

Myra Barker, *Gap, PA*

Quick & Easy Cheesy Chicken Casserole

Having company? This overnight dish can be popped in the oven right before guests arrive.

Serves 6 to 8

2 c. cooked chicken, diced
2 c. elbow macaroni, uncooked
2 c. milk
2 10 ¾-oz. cans cream of mushroom soup
2 onions, diced
8-oz. pkg. pasteurized process cheese spread, diced

Mix all ingredients together; spoon into an ungreased 13"x9" baking pan. Bake at 350 degrees for one hour. Or, refrigerate overnight and bake as directed right before serving.

Brittany Cornelius, *Chambersburg, PA*

Taco-Filled Pasta Shells

These beautiful little filled shells make a lovely dinner served with a fresh green salad.

Serves 8

2 lbs. ground beef
2 1¼-oz. pkgs. taco seasoning mix
8-oz. pkg. cream cheese, cubed
2 12-oz. pkgs. jumbo pasta shells, uncooked
¼ c. butter, melted
1 c. salsa
1 c. taco sauce
1 c. shredded Cheddar cheese
1 c. shredded Monterey Jack cheese
1 ½ c. tortilla chips, crushed
Optional: sour cream, chopped green onions

Brown beef in a skillet over medium heat; drain. Add taco seasoning and cook according to package directions. Add cream cheese; stir to melt. Remove beef mixture to a bowl and chill for one hour. Meanwhile, cook pasta shells according to package directions; drain. Toss shells with butter. Fill each shell with 3 tablespoons of beef mixture. Spoon salsa into a greased 13"x9" baking pan; place shells on top of salsa and cover with taco sauce. Bake, covered, at 350 degrees for 30 minutes. Uncover, sprinkle with cheeses and tortilla chips. Bake for 15 minutes, or until heated through.

Taco-Filled Pasta Shells

Susan Biffignani, *Fenton, MO*

Inside-Out Ravioli

Just add a crisp tossed salad with oil & vinegar dressing for a hearty Italian-style meal. Please pass the Parmesan!

Makes 10 servings

16-oz. pkg. small shell or bowtie pasta, uncooked
1 lb. ground beef
1 c. onion, chopped
½ c. dry bread crumbs
1 egg, beaten
1 t. Italian seasoning
1 t. salt
1 t. pepper
8-oz. pkg. sliced mushrooms
10-oz. pkg. frozen chopped spinach, thawed and drained
16-oz. jar spaghetti sauce
1 c. shredded mozzarella cheese
Garnish: grated Parmesan cheese

Cook pasta according to package directions; drain. Meanwhile, brown beef with onion in a skillet over medium heat; drain. In a greased 13"x9" baking pan, combine cooked pasta, beef mixture and remaining ingredients except sauce and cheeses. Stir gently; top with sauce and mozzarella cheese. Bake, uncovered, at 350 degrees for 45 minutes, or until hot and bubbly. Sprinkle with Parmesan cheese at serving time.

Michele Bartolomea, *Stafford, VA*

Spinach & Black Bean Lasagna

This vegetarian pasta dish is so delicious, no one will miss the meat!

Serves 9 to 12

2 eggs, beaten
16-oz. container ricotta cheese
10-oz. frozen spinach, thawed and drained
½ t. salt
¼ c. fresh cilantro, chopped
2 c. shredded Monterey Jack cheese
2 c. shredded Pepper Jack cheese
2 16-oz. cans black beans, drained and rinsed
2 13-oz. jars spaghetti sauce
½ t. ground cumin
12 strips no-boil lasagna noodles, uncooked

Mix eggs, ricotta cheese, spinach, salt and cilantro in a medium bowl; set aside. In a second bowl, combine Monterey Jack and Pepper Jack cheeses. Set aside. Mash beans with sauce and cumin in a third bowl; mix well. In a lightly greased 13"x9" baking pan, layer lasagna alternately with spinach mixture, cheese mixture and bean mixture, ending with remaining lasagna. Cover with aluminum foil and bake at 350 degrees for 45 minutes.

Spinach & Black Bean Lasagna

Carol Hickman, *Kingsport, TN*

Taco Lasagna

A hearty lasagna that's just a little different! It freezes well too, so it's a great make-ahead. Wrap the unbaked lasagna well and freeze up to three months. To serve, thaw overnight and bake as directed.

Makes 8 servings

12 lasagna noodles, uncooked
1 lb. ground beef chuck
1 ¼-oz. pkg. taco seasoning mix
2 egg whites, beaten
15-oz. container ricotta cheese
16-oz. pkg. finely shredded Colby Jack cheese, divided
24-oz. jar salsa, divided

Cook noodles according to package directions, just until tender; drain. Meanwhile, brown beef in a skillet over medium heat; drain. Stir in taco seasoning, adding a small amount of water if a thinner sauce is desired. Remove from heat. In a bowl, combine egg whites and ricotta cheese until well blended. Lightly spray a deep 13"x9" baking pan with non-stick vegetable spray. Layer 4 noodles, ¾ cup cheese mixture, half of beef mixture and 1 ⅓ cups shredded cheese. Next, layer with 4 noodles, ¾ cup cheese mixture, remaining beef mixture, 1 ½ cups salsa and 1 ⅓ cups shredded cheese. Layer with remaining noodles, cheese mixture, salsa and shredded cheese. Bake, uncovered, at 350 degrees for about 40 minutes, until hot and bubbly. Let stand for 10 minutes before serving.

Carol McKeon, *Lebanon, TN*

Cheddar Baked Spaghetti

This is my version of a dish my mother often made for us...it was our favorite Friday dinner. My brother and I still love it, as it always reminds us of Mom.

Serves 6 to 8

16-oz. pkg. thin spaghetti, uncooked
½ c. butter, softened
16-oz. jar double Cheddar cheese pasta sauce
12-oz. can tomato paste
2 T. sugar
⅓ c. Italian-flavored dry bread crumbs

Cook spaghetti according to package directions, just until tender. Drain; return to cooking pot. Add butter; toss spaghetti until butter melts. Stir in pasta sauce, tomato paste and sugar. Transfer to a greased 13"x9" baking pan; sprinkle with bread crumbs. Bake, uncovered, at 350 degrees for 35 minutes, or until bubbly and crunchy on top.

Cheddar Baked Spaghetti

Jo Ann, *Gooseberry Patch*

Chicken Lasagna with Roasted Red Pepper Sauce

There's nothing like a hot pan of lasagna on a cold winter's night! The Roasted Red Pepper Sauce is also great over your favorite noodles.

Serves 6 to 8

4 c. cooked chicken, finely chopped

2 8-oz. containers chive & onion cream cheese

10-oz. pkg. frozen chopped spinach, thawed and well drained

1 t. seasoned pepper

¾ t. garlic salt

9 no-boil lasagna noodles, uncooked

8-oz. pkg. shredded Italian 3-cheese blend

1 t. dried oregano

¼ t. pepper

Optional: sour cream, salsa

ROASTED RED PEPPER SAUCE:

12-oz. jar roasted red peppers, drained

16-oz. jar creamy Alfredo sauce

¾ c. grated Parmesan cheese

½ t. red pepper flakes

Stir together chicken, cream cheese, spinach and seasonings; set aside. Layer a lightly greased 13"x9" baking pan with ⅓ of Roasted Red Pepper Sauce, 3 noodles, ⅓ of chicken mixture and ⅓ of cheese. Repeat layers twice. Place baking pan on a baking sheet. Bake, covered, at 350 degrees for 50 to 55 minutes or until thoroughly heated. Uncover and bake 15 more minutes. Let rest 15 minutes before cutting.

Combine all ingredients in a blender; process until smooth.

> ~ **Cooking Tip** ~
>
> Buying boneless, skinless chicken breasts in bulk? Cook them all at once. Season with salt, pepper, and garlic, if desired, and allow to cool. Wrap tightly in plastic or place in a freezer bag. Kept in the freezer, they'll be ready for quick casseroles, sandwiches or zesty fajitas!

Chicken Lasagna with Roasted Red Pepper Sauce

Jenny Bishoff, *Mountain Lake Park, MD*

Meatball-Stuffed Shells

As a working mom with two little girls, I've found this super-easy recipe is great for a quick dinner. The kids can help too!

Serves 6 to 8

12-oz. pkg. jumbo pasta shells, uncooked
28-oz. jar pasta sauce, divided
36 frozen Italian meatballs, thawed
2 c. shredded mozzarella cheese
Garnish: grated Parmesan cheese

Cook pasta according to package directions; drain and rinse in cold water. Spread ½ cup pasta sauce in a greased 13"x9" baking pan. Tuck a meatball into each shell; arrange shells in pan. Top with remaining sauce; add cheese. Cover; bake at 350 degrees for 35 minutes. Uncover and bake 10 more minutes.

⟿ Cooking Tip ⟿

It's simple to swap fresh for dried herbs! For one teaspoon of a dried herb, simply substitute one tablespoon of the fresh herb.

Meatball-Stuffed Shells

April Bash, *Carlisle, PA*

Cheesy Chicken & Noodles

This recipe may seem like it has lots of ingredients, but it all comes together in one bowl and is baked in one pan. So easy!

Serves 8 to 10

12-oz. pkg. wide egg noodles, cooked
2 c. cooked chicken, cubed or shredded
2 10 ¾-oz. cans chicken noodle soup
10 ¾-oz. can cream of chicken soup
2 eggs, beaten
2 c. shredded Cheddar cheese
1 c. seasoned dry bread crumbs
1 t. garlic salt
1 t. onion salt
salt and pepper to taste

Combine all ingredients in a large bowl; mix well. Transfer to a lightly greased 13"x9" baking pan. Bake, uncovered, at 350 degrees for 35 to 40 minutes.

Diane Cohen, *Kennesaw, GA*

Lasagna Florentine

My family loves this beautiful lasagna. We have it at least once a month with fresh fruit.

Makes 9 servings

9 lasagna noodles, uncooked
1 lb. ground beef
½ c. onion, chopped
2 to 3 cloves garlic, minced
26-oz. jar spaghetti sauce, divided
16-oz. container cottage cheese
10-oz. pkg. frozen spinach, thawed and drained
12-oz. pkg. shredded mozzarella cheese, divided
½ c. grated Parmesan cheese, divided
2 eggs, beaten

Cook pasta according to package directions. Meanwhile, brown beef, onion and garlic. Drain; stir in spaghetti sauce and set aside. In a large bowl, combine cottage cheese, spinach, 2 cups mozzarella cheese, ¼ cup Parmesan cheese and eggs. In an ungreased 13"x9" baking pan, layer one cup sauce mixture, 3 noodles and ½ cup cottage cheese mixture; repeat layering once. Top with remaining 3 noodles, sauce mixture, mozzarella and Parmesan. Cover with aluminum foil; bake at 350 degrees for 30 minutes. Uncover; bake for an additional 15 minutes. Let stand for 10 minutes before serving.

Lasagna Florentine

Holly Sutton, *Middleburgh, NY*

Stuffed Pasta Shells

You'll have just enough time to make a crisp salad while this casserole is baking...it's ready in just 30 minutes.

Serves 6 to 8

18 jumbo pasta shells, uncooked
1½ c. chicken-flavored stuffing mix, cooked
2 c. cooked chicken, chopped
½ c. peas
½ c. mayonnaise
10 ¾-oz. can cream of chicken soup
⅔ c. water

Cook pasta shells according to package directions; drain. Meanwhile, combine stuffing, chicken, peas and mayonnaise; spoon into cooked pasta shells. Arrange shells in a greased 13"x9" baking pan. Mix soup and water; pour over shells. Cover and bake at 350 degrees for 30 minutes.

Colleen Leid, *Narvon, PA*

Company Baked Zita

With layers of sour cream and two kinds of cheese, this pasta classic is extra rich and cheesy. Try curly cavatappi or gemelli pasta instead of ziti too.

Serves 8

16-oz. pkg. ziti pasta, uncooked
1 lb. ground beef
1 lb. sweet Italian ground pork sausage
1 onion, chopped
2 26-oz. jars spaghetti sauce
16-oz. pkg. sliced provolone cheese
1 c. sour cream
1 ½ c. shredded mozzarella cheese
½ c. grated Parmesan cheese

Cook pasta according to package directions, just until tender; drain. Meanwhile, brown beef, sausage and onion in a skillet over medium heat; drain. Stir in sauce; reduce heat to low and simmer for 15 minutes. In a greased deep 13"x9" baking pan, layer half the cooked pasta, provolone cheese, sour cream, half the sauce mixture, remaining pasta, mozzarella cheese and remaining sauce. Top with Parmesan cheese. Cover and bake at 350 degrees for 30 minutes, or until hot, bubbly and cheeses are melted.

Company Baked Zita

Teresa Eller, *Tonganoxie, KS*

Busy-Day Spinach Lasagna

This lasagna recipe is easy to make because you don't have to cook the noodles ahead of time. Because you break up the noodles they fit nicely in the pan.

Makes 6 to 8 servings

1 ½ lbs. Italian sausage, browned and drained
2 T. Italian seasoning, divided
2 14-½ oz. cans diced tomatoes, drained
24-oz. jar spaghetti sauce, divided
6 c. fresh spinach, torn and divided
3 c. mozzarella cheese, divided
12-oz. pkg. lasagna noodles, uncooked, broken up and divided
Garnish: fresh basil

Spread sausage in the bottom of a 13"x9" baking pan sprayed with non-stick vegetable spray. Sprinkle with one tablespoon Italian seasoning. Add one can tomatoes with juice and half of spaghetti sauce; stir gently to combine. Add half of spinach; press down gently. Add one cup cheese and half of uncooked noodles. Repeat layers, starting with Italian seasoning and ending with cheese on top. Cover tightly with aluminum foil. Bake at 350 degrees for one hour, or until cooked through. Garnish with basil leaves.

Busy-Day Spinach Lasagna

***Judy Croll,** Rowlett, TX*

Aunt Judy's Baked Macaroni & Cheese

My family always requests this comforting dish for special holiday gatherings. It is so simple to prepare and delicious with baked ham or just by itself. There are never any leftovers.

Serves 8 to 10

8-oz. pkg. elbow macaroni,
    uncooked
2 T. oil
1 T. plus 1 t. salt, divided
¼ c. butter
⅓ c. all-purpose flour
3 c. milk, warmed
½ t. pepper
8-oz. pkg. pasteurized process
    cheese, cubed
½ c. shredded Cheddar cheese

Cook macaroni according to package directions, adding oil and one tablespoon salt to cooking water; drain and set aside. Meanwhile, melt butter in a large saucepan over medium heat. Add flour; cook and stir for 3 minutes, or until bubbly. Do not brown. Whisk in warm milk and bring to a boil, stirring constantly. Add remaining salt, pepper and cubed cheese. Stir until cheese is melted; remove from heat. Add cooked macaroni to cheese sauce and stir. Transfer to a buttered 3-quart casserole dish or 13"x9" baking pan. Bake, uncovered, at 350 degrees for 20 to 30 minutes, until bubbly. Top with shredded cheese; return to oven just until cheese melts. .

Cooking Tip

If you're adding more than one baking pan to the oven, remember to stagger them on the racks. Placing one pan directly over another won't allow the food to cook evenly.

Aunt Judy's Baked Macaroni & Cheese

Chapter Four

Main-Dish Favorites

Count down to dinner with these delicious recipes you can make in one pan. Pop Dijon Chicken & Fresh Herbs in the oven and serve with a fresh green salad for a satisfying meal. Want to make the entire meal in one pan? Italian Sausage & Potato Roast or Western Pork Chops have all the protein and veggies cooked in one pan. No need to fuss with lots of dishes. No matter what you choose to make, you can go from the oven to the table with a tasty meal they are sure to love!

Lori Rosenberg, *Cleveland, OH*

Pesto Polenta Lasagna

This vegetarian dish will please everyone! The polenta adds such a rich and creamy texture to this unusual lasagna.

Makes 8 servings

18-oz. tube polenta, sliced ¼-inch thick
   and divided
¼ c. basil pesto sauce, divided
1¼ c. marinara sauce, divided
1 c. shredded part-skim mozzarella cheese
¼ c. pine nuts

In a greased 13"x9" baking pan, arrange half of polenta slices in a single layer. Spread half of pesto over polenta; then spoon half of marinara. Repeat layering, ending with marinara sauce. Bake, uncovered, at 375 degrees for 25 minutes. Remove from oven; top with cheese and pine nuts. Place pan under a preheated broiler; broil until cheese is melted and nuts are toasted.

Diane Cohen, *Breinigsville, PA*

Italian Sausage & Potato Roast

So easy...everything is baked in one pan. Cooking the meat and veggies at a high temperature gives the meal a roasted flavor.

Makes 4 servings

¾ lb. redskin potatoes, cut into quarters
1 yellow pepper, sliced into strips
1 green pepper, sliced into strips
½ sweet onion, sliced
1 T. olive oil
1 t. garlic salt or garlic powder
¼ t. dried oregano
pepper to taste
1 lb. Italian pork sausage, cut into chunks

In a large bowl, toss vegetables with olive oil and seasonings. Line a large rimmed baking sheet with aluminum foil; lightly mist with non-stick vegetable spray. Spread into a 13"x9" baking pan, Place sausage chunks among vegetables. Bake, uncovered, at 450 degrees for about 30 minutes, until sausage is cooked through and vegetables are tender, stirring twice during baking.

Italian Sausage & Potato Roast

Vicki Holland, *Hampton, GA*

Baked Chicken Jambalaya

The sausage and chicken combine in this recipe to create a really yummy Southern dish that everyone loves!

Serves 8

1 lb. pkg. smoked beef sausage, sliced
¼ c. butter
4 c. cooked chicken, cubed
16-oz. pkg. frozen mixed vegetables, thawed
1 onion, sliced
4 stalks celery, sliced
1 green pepper, thinly sliced
2 c. shredded mozzarella or Cheddar cheese
16-oz. pkg. bowtie pasta, cooked

In a skillet over medium-high heat, sauté sausage in butter until browned. Add chicken to skillet with sausage. Transfer sausage mixture into a 13"x9" baking pan; add mixed vegetables, onion, celery and green pepper. Top with cheese and cover with aluminum foil. Bake at 350 degrees for about 30 minutes, or until veggies are crisp-tender and cheese is melted. Serve over pasta.

Kerry Mayer, *Dunham Springs, LA*

Western Pork Chops

For a delicious variation, try substituting peeled, cubed sweet potatoes for the redskins.

Serves 4

1 T. all-purpose flour
1 c. barbecue sauce
4 pork chops
salt and pepper to taste
4 redskin potatoes, sliced
1 green pepper, cubed
1 c. baby carrots

Shake flour in a large, plastic zipping bag. Add barbecue sauce to bag and squeeze bag to blend in flour. Season pork chops with salt and pepper; add pork chops to bag. Turn bag to coat pork chops with sauce. In a 13"x9" baking pan, arrange vegetables in an even layer. Remove pork chops from bag and place on top of vegetables. Cover with aluminum foil making a slit on the top. Bake at 350 degrees for about 40 to 45 minutes, until pork chops and vegetables are tender.

Western Pork Chops

Michelle Wittenberg, *Long Beach, CA*

Quick Pizza Casserole

If you like pepperoni pizza you'll love this casserole with all the pizza flavors.

Makes 4 to 6 servings

2 c. French bread, cubed and toasted
8-oz. jar pizza sauce
8-oz. container cottage cheese
1 c. shredded mozzarella cheese
4-oz. pkg. sliced pepperoni, halved
½ c. onion, chopped
½ t. dried basil
1 T. grated Parmesan cheese

In a large bowl, combine all ingredients except Parmesan cheese; blend well. Pour into a 13"x9" baking pan, Sprinkle Parmesan cheese over the top. Bake at 350 degrees for about 40 minutes, until hot.

Sheryl Eastman, *Wixom, MI*

Sausage & Apple Kraut

Serve with mashed potatoes, buttered green beans and fresh-baked rolls for a satisfying chilly-weather meal.

Makes 4 to 6 servings

27-oz. jar sauerkraut, drained, rinsed and
  divided
1 lb. Kielbasa sausage, sliced and divided
2 tart apples, peeled, cored and diced
½ c. brown sugar, packed and divided
2 c. apple cider or juice, divided

In a lightly greased 13"x9" baking pan, layer half of sauerkraut, half of sausage and all the apples. Sprinkle with ¼ cup brown sugar. Pour one cup cider or juice over top. Repeat layering. Cover and bake at 350 degrees for 1 ½ hours, or until sauerkraut is caramelized and golden.

⁓ Quick Tip ⁓

Keep hard grating cheeses like Parmesan fresh for longer. Wrap the cheese in a paper towel that has been moistened with cider vinegar, tuck into a plastic zipping bag and refrigerate.

Sausage & Apple Kraut

Gina McClenning, *Valrico, FL*

Tuscan Pork Loin

Guests always ask for this recipe. It makes a lot, but leftovers are delicious the next day. Instead of using plain cream cheese, try garlic-and-herb spreadable cheese.

Serves 10

3-lb. boneless pork tenderloin roast
8-oz. pkg. light cream cheese, softened
1 T. dried pesto seasoning
½ c. baby spinach
4 slices bacon, crisply cooked
12-oz. jar roasted red peppers, drained and divided
1 t. paprika
½ t. salt
½ t. pepper
Optional: baby spinach

Slice pork lengthwise, cutting down center, but not through other side. Open halves and cut down center of each half, cutting to, but not through other sides. Open pork into a rectangle. Place pork between 2 sheets of heavy-duty plastic wrap and flatten into an even thickness using a rolling pin or the flat side of a meat mallet. Spread cream cheese evenly over pork. Sprinkle with pesto seasoning; arrange spinach over cream cheese. Top with bacon slices and half of red peppers; reserve remaining red peppers for another recipe. Roll up pork lengthwise; tie at 2-inch intervals with kitchen string. Rub pork with paprika, salt and pepper. Place roast seam-side down on a lightly greased rack in a 13"x9" baking pan. Bake at 400 degrees for 50 minutes, or until a meat thermometer inserted into thickest portion registers 145 degrees. Remove from oven; let stand for 10 minutes. Remove string from pork; slice pork into ½-inch thick servings. Serve pork slices on a bed of spinach leaves, if desired.

Tuscan Pork Loin

Jackie Flood, *Geneseo, NY*

Pork Chop Potato Bake

The pork chops get so tender in this baked dish. We love it!

Serves 6

1 T. oil
6 boneless pork chops
seasoned salt and pepper to taste
1 c. shredded Cheddar cheese, divided
10 ³/₄-oz. can cream of mushroom soup
¹/₂ c. milk
¹/₂ c. sour cream
28-oz. pkg. frozen diced potatoes with onions
    and peppers, thawed
1 to 2 T. onion soup mix

Heat oil in a skillet over medium-high heat. Season pork chops with salt and pepper; brown in oil for 5 minutes per side, until golden. In a bowl, combine ¹/₂ cup cheese and remaining ingredients. Spread mixture in a greased 3-quart casserole dish or 13"x9" baking pan,. Arrange pork chops over top of mixture. Bake, covered, at 350 degrees for 40 minutes. Top with remaining cheese. Bake, uncovered, for an additional 10 minutes, or until cheese is melted.

Michelle Waddington, *New Bedford, MA*

Baked Crumbed Haddock

Delicious! Serve with mac & cheese and steamed broccoli for a down-home dinner.

Serves 4

5 ¹/₂-oz. pkg. onion & garlic croutons
4 T. butter, melted
2 lbs. haddock fillets
Optional: lemon slices

Finely grind croutons in a food processor. Toss together croutons and butter. Place fish in a lightly greased 13"x9" baking pan. Sprinkle crouton mixture over fish. Bake, uncovered, at 350 degrees for 20 to 25 minutes, until fish flakes easily with a fork. Top fish with lemon slices, if desired.

> ### ∼ Quick Tip ∼
> An easy clean-up after baking fish...just pour white vinegar into the hot baking pan and let sit several minutes before cleaning.

Baked Crumbed Haddock

Laurie Patton, *Pinckney, MI*

Laurie's Stuffed Peppers

This no-meat dish is a favorite of ours! I serve it with a fresh green salad.

Makes 4 servings

4 small green, red or yellow
   peppers
1 T. extra-virgin olive oil
8-oz. pkg. mushrooms, finely
   chopped
1 onion, finely chopped
1 stalk celery, diced
1 clove garlic, minced
1 c. brown rice, cooked
¼ t. hot pepper sauce
¼ t. salt
¼ t. pepper
15-oz. can tomato sauce,
   divided
¾ c. shredded mozzarella
   cheese
Optional: fresh thyme sprigs

Slice off tops of peppers; remove seeds. Fill a large soup pot with water; bring water to a boil over medium-high heat. Add peppers; boil 5 minutes. Remove peppers; set aside. Heat oil in a large skillet over medium heat; add mushrooms, onion, celery and garlic. Sauté 5 minutes or until onion is tender. Add rice, hot pepper sauce, salt and pepper; cook 2 minutes. Add half of the tomato sauce and simmer 5 minutes; spoon into peppers. Spread remaining tomato sauce into an ungreased 13"x9" baking pan. Place filled peppers in pan. Bake, uncovered, at 350 degrees for 25 minutes; sprinkle with cheese. Bake 10 more minutes or until cheese is melted. Garnish with thyme sprigs, if desired.

> ### ⸺ Cooking Tip ⸺
> Garlic is easily minced when you smash the clove, still in the peel, with the side of a knife blade. The peel will come right off, and the clove will be flat and easy to chop!

Laurie's Stuffed Peppers

Dawn Henning, *Hilliard, OH*

Potato Puff Casserole

This is the kids' favorite casserole, but all the adults like it too!

Serves 6 to 8

1 lb. ground beef
10 ¾-oz. can cream of mushroom soup
3 14 ½-oz. cans green beans, drained
12 slices pasteurized process cheese spread
16-oz. pkg. frozen potato puffs

In a skillet over medium heat, brown beef; drain and stir in soup. Pour beef mixture into a greased 13"x9" baking pan. Top with green beans and sliced cheese. Arrange a single layer of potato puffs over cheese. Cover with aluminum foil and bake at 400 degrees for 20 minutes, or until cheese is melted. Uncover and bake again for 10 minutes, or until potato puffs are golden.

Amy Butcher, *Columbus, GA*

Garlicky Baked Shrimp

Here's the perfect party recipe...guests peel their own shrimp and save you the work!

Serves 6

2 lbs. uncooked large shrimp, cleaned and
    unpeeled
16-oz. bottle light Italian salad dressing
1½ T. pepper
2 cloves garlic, pressed
2 lemons, halved
¼ c. fresh parsley, chopped
2 T. butter, cut into small pieces

Place shrimp, salad dressing, pepper and garlic in an ungreased 13"x9" baking pan, tossing to coat. Squeeze juice from lemons over shrimp mixture; stir. Cut lemon halves into wedges and add to pan. Sprinkle shrimp with parsley; dot with butter. Bake, uncovered, at 375 degrees for 25 minutes, stirring after 15 minutes. Serve in pan.

Garlicky Baked Shrimp

Jo Ann, *Gooseberry Patch*

Tangy Citrus Chicken

The molasses in this dish gives it a rich brown color and sweet flavor.

Makes 8 servings

8 boneless, skinless chicken breasts
6-oz. can frozen lemonade, thawed
¾ c. molasses
1 t. dried savory
½ t. ground mustard
½ t. dried thyme
1 t. lemon juice

Place chicken in a 13"x9" baking pan coated with non-stick vegetable spray. In a medium mixing bowl, combine remaining ingredients; mix well. Pour half of the mixture over the chicken. Bake, uncovered, at 350 degrees for 20 minutes. Turn chicken; add remaining sauce. Bake an additional 15 to 20 minutes, or until juices run clear.

Penny Sherman, *Ava, MO*

South-of-the-Border Chicken

Scrumptious...makes any meal a fiesta!

Makes 4 servings

2 T. all-purpose flour
14 ½-oz. can diced tomatoes with chili seasoning
2 t. jalapeños, diced
½ t. salt
15-oz. can black beans, drained and rinsed
6 boneless, skinless chicken breasts
1 yellow pepper, sliced

Shake flour in a large oven bag; place bag in a 13"x9" baking pan. Add tomatoes, jalapeños and salt to bag; squeeze to blend with flour. Add beans and chicken to bag; turn to coat chicken. Top with yellow pepper. Close bag with nylon tie provided; cut six, ½-inch slits in top. Bake at 350 degrees for 45 to 50 minutes, until chicken juices run clear.

South-of-the-Border Chicken

Alma Meyers, *Guernsey, WY*

Quick Salisbury Steak

Add a side of mashed potatoes for a hearty, filling dinner.

Makes 4 servings

1 lb. ground beef
1 ½-oz. pkg. onion soup mix
2 eggs, beaten
2 10 ¾-oz. cans golden mushroom soup

In a large bowl, combine beef, soup mix and eggs; mix well and form into 4 patties. Place patties in an ungreased 13"x9" baking pan; cover with soup. Bake at 350 degrees for 35 minutes, or until patties are no longer pink in the center.

Erin Hibshman, *Lebanon, PA*

No-Fuss Chicken Dinner

Perfect for those busy days when you need a good meal with easy clean-up. This is all made in one pan and cooks in about an hour.

Makes 4 to 6 servings

4 to 6 boneless, skinless chicken breasts, cut into strips
4 baking potatoes, quartered
½ lb. baby carrots
1 onion, chopped
10 ¾-oz. can cream of chicken soup
¼ t. garlic powder
2 to 4 T. water

Place chicken in the bottom of a 13"x9" baking pan. Arrange vegetables around chicken. In a bowl, stir together soup, garlic powder and enough water to make it pourable. Spoon soup mixture over chicken and vegetables. Cover and bake at 350 degrees for about one hour, until chicken is done and potatoes and carrots are tender.

No-Fuss Chicken Dinner

Linda Diepholz, *Lakeville, MN*

Baked Chicken Chimichangas

I have been making these chicken chimis for years. I like that they are baked and not deep-fried...much healthier. People who don't even like Mexican food discover they love these. I make this recipe often and I even like the leftovers cold!

Serves 4 to 6

1 ½ c. cooked chicken, chopped
    or shredded
¾ c. salsa or picante sauce
1 ½ c. shredded Cheddar cheese
3 green onions, chopped
1 t. ground cumin
1 t. dried oregano
6 8-inch flour tortillas
2 T. butter, melted
Garnish: additional shredded
    cheese, green onions, salsa

In a bowl, combine chicken, salsa or sauce, cheese, onions and seasonings. Spoon ⅓ cup of mixture down the center of each tortilla; fold opposite sides over filling. Roll up from bottom and place seam-side down in a greased 13"x9" baking pan. Brush with melted butter. Bake, uncovered, at 400 degrees for 30 minutes or until golden, turning halfway through cooking. Garnish with additional cheese and onions; serve with salsa on the side, as desired.

~ **Quick Tip** ~
Keep cutting boards smelling fresh by simply rubbing them thoroughly with lemon wedges. Works for hands too!

Baked Chicken Chimichangas

Lisa Ashton, *Aston, PA*

White Cheddar-Cauliflower Casserole

Lots of cheese and bacon will have the kids eating their cauliflower in this terrific casserole.

Serves 6

1 head cauliflower, cooked and mashed
8-oz. pkg. shredded white Cheddar cheese, divided
½ lb. bacon, crisply cooked, crumbled and divided
½ c. cream cheese, softened
2 T. sour cream
salt and pepper to taste

Combine cauliflower, half the Cheddar cheese and ¾ of the bacon in a bowl. Add cream cheese and sour cream; mix well. Spread mixture in a greased 8"x8" baking pan; top with remaining Cheddar cheese and bacon. Sprinkle with salt and pepper. Bake, uncovered, at 350 degrees for 20 to 25 minutes, until bubbly and golden around edges.

Margaret Vinci, *Pasadena, CA*

Momma's Divine Divan

Choose rotisserie chicken from your supermarket deli to add more flavor to this family favorite. Generally, one rotisserie chicken will yield 3 cups of chopped meat, so you'll need 2 rotisserie chickens to get the 4 to 5 cups needed for this recipe. Add cooked rice, and you have a complete meal!

Serves 8 to 10

½ lb. broccoli flowerets, cooked
4 boneless, skinless chicken breasts, cooked and cubed
salt to taste
1 c. seasoned dry bread crumbs
1 T. butter, melted
10 ¾-oz. can cream of chicken soup
½ c. mayonnaise
1 t. curry powder
½ t. lemon juice
1 c. shredded Cheddar cheese

Arrange broccoli in a lightly greased 13"x9" baking pan. Sprinkle chicken with salt to taste; place on top of broccoli and set aside. Toss together bread crumbs and butter; set aside. Combine soup, mayonnaise, curry powder and lemon juice in a separate bowl; spread over chicken and broccoli. Top with cheese; sprinkle with bread crumb mixture. Bake, uncovered, at 350 degrees for 25 minutes, or until hot and bubbly.

Momma's Divine Divan

Main-Dish Favorites

Jo Ann, *Gooseberry Patch*

Speedy Steak & Veggies

This recipe makes a complete meal and everyone thinks it is so special!

Serves 4 to 6

juice of 1 lime
salt and pepper to taste
1 ½ lb. beef flank steak
½ bunch broccoli, cut into flowerets
2 c. baby carrots, sliced
2 ears corn, husked and cut into 2-inch pieces
1 red onion, sliced into wedges
2 T. olive oil

Combine lime juice, salt and pepper; brush over both sides of beef. Place on a broiler pan and broil, 5 minutes per side, turning once. Set aside on a cutting board; keep warm. Toss broccoli, carrots, corn and onion with oil. Spoon onto a lightly greased 13"x9" baking pan, Bake at 400 degrees, turning once, until tender, about 20 minutes. Slice the steak into thin strips on the diagonal and arrange on a platter. Surround with vegetables.

Stacie Avner, *Delaware, OH*

Dijon Chicken & Fresh Herbs

I love making this family favorite in the summertime with my fresh garden herbs.

Serves 6

4 boneless, skinless chicken breasts
2 T. olive oil
½ t. kosher salt
1 t. pepper
3 to 4 T. Dijon mustard
2 T. fresh rosemary, minced
2 T. fresh thyme, minced
2 T. fresh parsley, minced

Sprinkle chicken with salt and pepper. In a heavy skillet, brown the chicken over medium-high heat in olive oil for about 5 minutes per side. Remove from skillet and place in a 13"x9" baking pan Brush with mustard and herbs. Cover and bake at 350 degrees for about 30 minutes until juices run clear.

Dijon Chicken & Fresh Herbs

Kristie Rigo, *Friedens, PA*

Oven Beef & Noodles

Our family loves beef & noodles and this is the quickest and yummiest recipe I have found. The entire family loves it and I love that it is so easy to clean up!

Makes 6 to 8 serving

1 ¹/₂-oz. pkg. onion soup mix
4 c. water
10 ³/₄-oz. can cream of mushroom soup
2 ¹/₂-lb. boneless beef chuck roast
12-oz. pkg. kluski egg noodles, uncooked

Combine soup mix and water in a 13"x9" baking pan; stir in soup. Place roast in pan on top of soup mixture. Cover and bake at 350 degrees for 3 hours, or until roast is very tender. Remove roast from pan and shred; return to pan. Add noodles to pan; reduce heat to 300 degrees. Cover and bake for 20 to 30 minutes, stirring every 15 minutes until noodles are tender. Add water if necessary to prevent drying out.

Linda Strausburg, *Arroyo Grande, CA*

Bacon-Wrapped Chicken

Each chicken breast is coated with herb-flavored cream cheese, rolled up and wrapped in bacon, making this dish an excellent choice for special get-togethers.

Serves 2

2 boneless, skinless chicken breasts, flattened
   to ¹/₂-inch thickness
¹/₂ t. salt
¹/₄ t. pepper
2 T. chive-and-onion-flavored cream cheese,
   softened and divided
2 T. chilled butter, divided
¹/₂ t. dried tarragon, divided
2 slices bacon

Sprinkle chicken with salt and pepper. Spread one tablespoon cream cheese over each chicken breast; top with one tablespoon butter and ¹/₄ teaspoon tarragon. Roll up and wrap with one slice bacon; secure with a toothpick. Place chicken seam-side down in 13"x9" baking pan. Bake at 400 degrees for 30 minutes or until juices run clear when chicken is pierced with a fork. Increase temperature to broil. Watching the broiler carefully, broil 8 to 10 minutes or just until bacon is crisp.

Bacon-Wrapped Chicken

Tegan Reeves, *Auburndale, FL*

Crunchy Corn Chip Chicken

Dinner in a jiffy...so quick to whip up!

Makes 6 servings

6 boneless, skinless chicken breasts
10 ¾-oz. can cream of chicken soup
8-oz. pkg. shredded Cheddar cheese, divided
1 ¼-oz. pkg. taco seasoning mix
2 c. barbecue corn chips, crushed

Arrange chicken in an ungreased 13"x9" baking pan; set aside. Combine soup, one cup cheese and taco seasoning together; spread over chicken. Bake, uncovered, at 450 degrees for 45 minutes; sprinkle with corn chips and remaining cheese. Return to oven; bake until cheese melts, about 5 minutes.

Jodi Zarnoth-Hirsch, *Chilton, WI*

Cranberry Meatloaves

This favorite comfort-food recipe is dressed up with a yummy cranberry topping.

Serves 5

1 lb. lean ground beef
1 c. cooked rice
½ c. tomato juice
¼ c. onion, minced
1 egg, beaten
1 t. salt
14-oz. can whole-berry cranberry sauce
⅓ c. brown sugar, packed
1 T. lemon juice

Mix together ground beef, rice, tomato juice, onion, egg and salt. Shape mixture evenly into 5 mini meatloaves and place in a greased 13"x9" baking pan. Mix together cranberry sauce, brown sugar and lemon juice; spoon over top of each loaf. Bake at 350 degrees for 45 minutes.

Cranberry Meatloaves

Cris Goode, Morresville, IN

Good & Healthy "Fried" Chicken

We love this healthier version of everyone's favorite food...fried chicken!

Makes 4 servings

1 c. whole-grain panko bread crumbs
1 c. cornmeal
2 T. all-purpose flour
salt and pepper to taste
1 c. buttermilk
8 chicken drumsticks

Combine panko, cornmeal, flour, salt and pepper in a gallon-size plastic zipping bag. Coat chicken with buttermilk, one piece at a time. Drop chicken into bag and shake to coat pieces lightly. Arrange chicken in a 13"x9" baking pan,baking pan coated with non-stick vegetable spray. Bake, uncovered, at 350 degrees for 40 to 50 minutes, until chicken juices run clear.

Mary Kathryn Carter, Platte City, MO

Cream Cheese Enchiladas

This creamy variation on Mexican enchiladas is yummy! It won me 1st place in a local newspaper's holiday cooking contest. For a brunch twist, use breakfast sausage instead of ground beef.

Makes 8 servings

8-oz. pkg. cream cheese, softened
1 c. sour cream
10-oz. can mild green chile enchilada sauce
¼ c. jalapeños, chopped
1 lb. ground beef, browned and drained
½ c. shredded sharp Cheddar cheese
8 8-inch flour tortillas
1 sweet onion, chopped
½ c. sliced black olives
Garnish: sliced black olives, chopped tomato, shredded lettuce, chopped green onions

Blend together cream cheese, sour cream, enchilada sauce and jalapeños in a large bowl; set aside. Combine ground beef and shredded cheese in another bowl; set aside. Fill each tortilla with one to 2 tablespoons cream cheese mixture and one to 2 tablespoons beef mixture. Sprinkle each with onion and olives; roll up tortillas. Place in a 13"x9" baking pan; cover with remaining cream cheese mixture. Bake, uncovered, at 400 degrees for 30 to 40 minutes; cover if top begins to brown. Garnish with olives, tomatoes, lettuce and green onions.

Cream Cheese Enchiladas

Main-Dish Favorites

Gloria Robertson, *Midland, TX*

Spinach Soufflé

This is an impressive dish but is so easy to make. It cuts beautifully and everyone thinks you have spent the whole day in the kitchen.

Makes 6 servings

10-oz. pkg. frozen, chopped spinach, thawed
3 T. all-purpose flour
3 eggs, beaten
½ t. salt
12-oz. container cottage cheese
1 c. shredded Cheddar cheese
¼ c. butter, melted

In a large mixing bowl, combine spinach with flour; add eggs, salt, cottage cheese, Cheddar cheese and butter. Place in a greased 13"x9" baking pan. Bake, covered, at 375 degrees for 45 minutes. Uncover and bake an additional 15 minutes.

Jennifer Holmes, *Philadelphia, PA*

Fruity Baked Chicken

Serve over rice with a side of asparagus spears...yum!

Makes 6 servings

2 T. olive oil
6 4-oz. boneless, skinless chicken breasts
3 lemons, halved
3 oranges, halved
1 apple, peeled, cored and chopped

Coat the bottom of a 13"x9" baking pan with olive oil; arrange chicken breasts on top. Squeeze juice from one lemon and one orange over chicken; set aside. Slice remaining lemons and oranges into wedges; cut these in half. Arrange around and on top of chicken breasts; add apple. Cover and bake at 350 degrees for one hour and 45 minutes; uncover for last 30 minutes of baking.

> **Cooking Tip**
> No peeking! When baking any dish, the temperature drops 25 degrees every time the oven door is opened.

Fruity Baked Chicken

Chapter Five

Sandwiches, Wraps & Pizza

Make those light meals just right with recipes that bake in flavor and leave little clean-up. Spicy Italian Roast Beef Sliders and tasty Seaside Salmon Buns are quickly assembled and then baked in the oven for some extra goodness. Love to serve pizza, but want it quick & easy? Try a rich White Chicken Pizza or a clever BLT Pizza that will please them all. Need a hot sandwich for after the game? Mama's Quick Meatball Subs are the perfect choice! So go ahead and fix that easy homemade meal they are sure to enjoy.

Michelle Schuberg, *Big Rapids, MI*

White Chicken Pizza

A quick & easy dinner even your most picky eater will love!

Serves 8

**13.8-oz. can refrigerated pizza
   crust dough**
1 T. olive oil
**2 boneless, skinless chicken
   breasts, cubed**
2 T. garlic, minced
16-oz. jar Alfredo pasta sauce
¼ c. onion, chopped
**8-oz. pkg. shredded mozzarella,
   Parmesan & Romano cheese
   blend**

Spread dough onto a lightly greased 13"x9" baking pan; bake at 425 degrees for 7 minutes. Heat oil in a skillet over medium heat; sauté chicken and garlic in oil until juices run clear when chicken is pierced. Pour Alfredo sauce over baked crust; sprinkle with chicken and onion. Bake 10 more minutes; top with cheese blend and return to oven until cheeses melt.

White Chicken Pizza

Linda Peterson, *Mason, MI*

Turkey, Black Bean & Sweet Potato Tacos

Bored with the same ol' tacos? These are packed with delicious fresh ingredients! Any leftover filling can be frozen for another meal.

Makes 8 to 10 servings

1 lb. ground turkey
2 T. taco seasoning mix
1/2 c. tomato sauce
15-oz. can black beans, drained and rinsed
3 sweet potatoes, peeled and diced
2 T. butter, sliced
1 1/2 c. fresh spinach, chopped
1 1/2 c. shredded Cheddar cheese
8 to 10 corn taco shells
Garnish: sour cream, salsa, guacamole

Brown turkey in a skillet over medium-high heat; drain. Stir in taco seasoning, tomato sauce and beans; set aside. In a lightly greased 13"x9" baking pan, layer as follows: sweet potatoes, sliced butter, spinach, turkey mixture and cheese. Cover with aluminum foil. Bake at 375 degrees for 45 minutes, or until sweet potatoes are tender. Serve spooned into taco shells, garnished as desired.

Audrey Lett, *Newark, DE*

Suzanne's Tomato Melt

I love this as a quick breakfast with a cup of coffee...it is so easy to make!

Makes one serving

1 onion bagel or English muffin, split
1/4 c. shredded Cheddar cheese
2 tomato slices
1 T. grated Parmesan cheese
several fresh basil leaves

Place bagel or English muffin halves in a 13"x9" baking pan, cut-sides up. Sprinkle each with half of the Cheddar cheese. Top with a tomato slice. Sprinkle half the Parmesan cheese over each tomato. Add fresh basil leaf on top. Bake at 425 degrees for about 10 minutes, or until cheese is bubbly.

Suzanne's Tomato Melt

Lydia McCormick, *Burkburnett, TX*

Seaside Salmon Buns

Using canned salmon makes these yummy sandwiches super quick & easy! But if you have leftover grilled or baked salmon, the sandwich is very rich and tasty. Either choice is a good one!

Serves 6

14-oz. can salmon, drained and
    flaked or 1 c. grilled or baked
    salmon, chopped
¼ c. green pepper, chopped
1 T. onion, chopped
2 t. lemon juice
½ c. mayonnaise
6 pretzel buns, split
½ c. shredded Cheddar cheese

Mix salmon, pepper, onion, lemon juice and mayonnaise. Pile salmon mixture onto bottom bun halves; sprinkle with cheese. Arrange salmon-topped buns in a 13"x9" baking pan. Bake at 400 degrees for about 15 minutes, until lightly golden and cheese is melted. Top with remaining bun halves. Bake for 10 more minutes. Serve immediately.

⎯ Cooking Tip ⎯
If using canned salmon, choose the highest quality available and remove any bones or skin that may be in the can.

Seaside Salmon Buns

Roger Dahlstrom, *Ankeny, IA*

Italian Roast Beef Sliders

These sliders are so quick to assemble and baking them for just a few minutes is the perfect way to blend all the wonderful flavors.

Serves 12

12 3-inch slider rolls, split
12 oz. thinly sliced deli-style
   roast beef
1½ c. pickled mixed vegetables
   such as giardiniera, chopped
6 oz. sliced provolone cheese
1 8-oz. container cream
   cheese spread with garden
   vegetables
¼ c. olive oil
1 t. Italian seasoning
½ t. red pepper flakes

Arrange bottoms of rolls in a 13"x9" baking pan. Layer roll bottoms with roast beef, pickled mixed vegetables and provolone. Spread cut sides of roll tops with cream cheese. Add roll tops. In a bowl, combine the remaining ingredients. Drizzle over rolls. Cover pan with aluminum foil. Bake at 350 degrees for 15 minutes. Uncover; bake 10 to 15 minutes more, or until cheese is melted and roll tops are lightly golden.

> ## ⟶ Quick Tip ⟵
> If you prefer turkey or chicken instead of beef, deli-style mesquite turkey or chicken is a great substitute. Hot-pepper cheese with onion rolls makes a great combination with the turkey or chicken.

Italian Roast Beef Sliders

Anne Alesauskas, *Minocqua, WI*

BLT Pizza

If you like BLT sandwiches, you will love this tasty cool pizza. We like to serve it in the summertime on hot evenings with a glass of lemonade.

Serves 10 to 12

8-oz. tube refrigerated crescent rolls
¾ c. mayonnaise
1 T. Dijon mustard
9 slices bacon, crisply cooked and crumbled
8-oz. pkg. shredded Cheddar cheese
2 green onions, finely chopped
2 to 3 c. lettuce, shredded
3 roma tomatoes, seeded and chopped

Roll out crescent rolls in a lightly greased 13"x9" baking pan, pinching seams to seal. Bake at 375 degrees for 12 to 15 minutes, until lightly golden. Remove from oven; cool. In a small bowl, combine mayonnaise and mustard; spread over crescent rolls. Top with remaining ingredients. Cut into squares.

∼ Quick Tip ∼
Add some garden favorites such as sliced cucumbers, blanched asparagus, fresh spinach or thinly sliced carrots to this pizza.

BLT Pizza

Carol Lytle, *Columbus, OH*

Ham Sandwich Supreme

This easy sandwich is always welcome at potlucks, tailgating parties and other get-togethers. One sandwich will not be enough! A friend shared this recipe with me.

Makes 12 sandwiches

1 doz. brown & serve rolls, split
½ lb. sliced deli baked ham
12 slices provolone cheese
½ c. butter
2 T. brown sugar, packed
1 T. Worcestershire sauce
1 T. mustard
Optional: 1 T. poppy seed

Assemble 12 sandwiches with rolls, ham and cheese. Arrange sandwiches in a lightly buttered 13"x9" baking pan; set aside. Combine remaining ingredients in a small saucepan over medium heat. Bring to a boil, stirring until brown sugar dissolves; spoon over sandwiches. Bake, uncovered, at 350 degrees for 10 to 30 minutes, until crisp and golden on top.

Christine Gordon, *Rapid City, SD*

French Bread Pizza Burgers

A quick & easy dinner...kids will love to eat this as much as they'll love helping Mom make it! Change it up any way you like, adding other pizza toppings to your own taste.

Serves 6 to 8

1 loaf French bread, halved lengthwise
15-oz. can pizza sauce
1 lb. ground pork sausage, browned and drained
3½-oz. pkg. sliced pepperoni
8-oz. pkg. shredded mozzarella cheese

Place both halves of loaf on an ungreased 13"x9" baking pan cut sides up. Spread with pizza sauce; top with sausage, pepperoni and cheese. Bake at 350 degrees for 15 minutes, or until cheese is melted. Slice to serve.

French Bread Pizza Burgers

Tara Horton, *Delaware, OH*

Black Bean & Rice Enchiladas

Using fresh cilantro in this recipe is the best!

Makes 8 servings

1 green pepper, chopped
¼ c. onion, chopped
3 cloves garlic, minced
1 T. olive oil
15-oz. can black beans, drained
    and rinsed
14¼-oz. can diced tomatoes
    with green chiles
¼ c. taco sauce
1 T. chili powder
1 t. ground cumin
¼ t. red pepper flakes
2 c. cooked brown rice
8 10-inch multi-grain flour
    tortillas
1 c. salsa
½ c. shredded Cheddar cheese
3 T. fresh cilantro, chopped

In a skillet over medium heat, sauté green pepper, onion and garlic in oil until tender. Add beans, tomatoes, taco sauce and seasonings. Simmer until heated through and mixture thickens. Add rice; cook 5 minutes. Spoon filling down the center of each tortilla. Roll up tortillas; place in a lightly greased 13"x9" baking pan. Spoon salsa over tortillas. Bake, covered, at 350 degrees for 25 minutes. Uncover; sprinkle with cheese and cilantro. Bake an additional 3 minutes, or until cheese is melted.

~ Quick Tip ~

If you want to add more protein to this dish, brown some ground beef and mix with the beans and tomato mixture before adding to the tortillas.

Black Bean & Rice Enchiladas

Delores Begansky, *Wilmington, CT*

Garlic & Mustard Burgers

No one will be able to resist these tasty burgers! Placing the grilled burgers in the oven for just a few minutes makes the cheese melt just right.

Serves 4

1 lb. ground beef
3 T. country-style Dijon
    mustard
4 cloves garlic, chopped
4 slices Monterey Jack cheese
7-oz. jar roasted red peppers,
    drained
4 hamburger buns, split and
    toasted

Mix together beef, mustard and garlic. Shape mixture into 4 patties about ¾-inch thick. Cover and grill patties for 12 to 15 minutes, to desired doneness. Top with cheese and peppers. Place on toasted buns and put in 13"x9" baking pan. Bake at 350 degrees until cheese is melted, about 10 minutes. Serve immediately.

> ── **Quick Tip** ──
> Choose wood cutting boards to use as serving trays to present your sandwiches. Place a sheet of natural-color parchment paper under each sandwich.

Garlic & Mustard Burgers

Cris Goode, *Mooresville, IN*

Mama's Quick Meatball Subs

We like to serve our meatball subs open-faced. That way we get more of the yummy meatballs and can add lots of sauce and cheese!

Serves 4

1 lb. extra-lean ground beef
20 saltine crackers, crushed
12-oz. bottle chili sauce, divided
¼ c. grated Parmesan cheese
2 egg whites, beaten
salt and pepper to taste
15-oz. jar pizza sauce, warmed
2 loaves French baguette, halved and split
2 c. favorite shredded cheese

Combine beef, cracker crumbs, half of chili sauce, Parmesan cheese, egg whites, salt and pepper in a bowl. Mix well; form into 12, 1½ inch meatballs. Place in a 13"x9" baking pan sprayed with non-stick vegetable spray. Bake at 400 degrees for 20 minutes, or until cooked through, turning meatballs halfway through. Add baked meatballs to warmed sauce. Fill each half-loaf with 3 meatballs and sprinkle with cheese. Place on a baking sheet and heat for another 10 minutes or until cheese is melted and golden. Serve open-face or with tops on. Serve with remaining chili sauce on the side.

> ~ **Quick Tip** ~
>
> If time is short, you can mix up and cook the meatballs the day before. Keep refrigerated until you are ready to assemble the sandwich.

Mama's Quick Meatball Subs

Nancy Kremkus, *Ann Arbor, MI*

Pepperoni Pizza Bites

Get creative and try this recipe with alternative toppings...you'll have a blast! So fun to make with the kids.

Makes 8 mini pizzas

11-oz. tube refrigerated thin pizza crust
½ c. pizza sauce
8 slices pepperoni
½ c. shredded mozzarella cheese

Do not unroll pizza crust; cut into 8 equal pieces. Arrange dough 2 inches apart in a greased 13"x9" baking pan. Flatten each piece of dough into a 2-inch circle. Spoon pizza sauce into each center. Top each pizza with pepperoni and cheese. Bake at 400 degrees for 12 minutes or until golden and cheese melts.

Jo Ann, *Gooseberry Patch*

Veggie Melts

We love to use a crusty bread like ciabatta for these sandwiches because it has so much texture. If you like the bread softer, brush with olive oil before baking.

Makes 4 servings

1 c. sliced baby portabella mushrooms
¼ c. olive oil
1 loaf ciabatta bread, halved horizontally
8-oz. jar whole roasted red peppers, drained
1½ t. Italian seasoning
1 c. shredded Fontina cheese

In a skillet over medium heat, sauté mushrooms in olive oil until tender. Place bread halves on a flat surface. On one bread half, layer peppers and mushrooms. Add Italian seasoning and cheese. Assemble sandwich and cut into 4 pieces. Place in a 13"x9" baking pan. Bake in a 350 degree oven for 15 minutes until cheese is melted. Serve immediately.

Veggie Melts

Jennifer Oglesby, Brookville, IN

Garden-Fresh Pesto Pizza

With this easy pizza, you can really taste what summer is all about! I came up with this recipe last summer when I had a bounty of cherry tomatoes and fresh basil.

Makes 8 servings

12-inch pizza crust
⅓ c. basil pesto
½ c. shredded mozzarella
　cheese
1½ c. cherry tomatoes, halved
Optional: 4 leaves fresh basil

Place crust and stretch into a lightly greased 13"x9" baking pan. Spread pesto over pizza crust and top with cheese. Scatter tomatoes over cheese; add a basil leaf to each quarter of the pizza, if desired. Bake at 425 degrees for about 8 to 10 minutes, until crust is crisp and cheese is lightly golden. Cut into wedges or squares.

∽ Quick Tip ∽

If you love cherry tomatoes and have plenty, serve them on a round plate, placing the tomatoes around the edge. Add fresh veggies in the middle.

Garden-Fresh Pesto Pizza

Henry Burnley, *Ankeny, IA*

Pick-Me-Up Mini Pizzas

These little pizzas are quick to make and easy to pick up and eat. Serve as an appetizer or add some fresh fruit or a green salad for a quick meal.

Serves 12

1½ c. all-purpose flour
¾ c. cornmeal
2 T. sugar
½ t. baking powder
½ t. salt
1 egg
¼ c. water
2 T. olive oil
¾ c. pizza sauce
½ c. mini pepperoni slices
1½ c. finely shredded
   mozzarella or Italian-blend
   cheese

In a small bowl, mix flour, cornmeal, sugar, baking powder and salt. In another small bowl, beat together egg, water and oil. Add egg mixture to flour mixture and mix well. Add more water if necessary to form a ball. Divide dough into 12 pieces; form into balls and place in shallow 13"x9" baking pans. Using your fingers, press each ball of dough into a round flat shape. Spread each crust with one tablespoon pizza sauce. Top with pepperoni. Sprinkle each with 2 tablespoons of cheese. Bake at 375 degrees for 10 minutes. Increase oven temperature to 400 degrees and bake about 10 minutes more until crust begins to brown and cheese is melted and golden.

> **⟨⟩ Quick Tip ⟨⟩**
>
> If you like, add other toppings to these easy-to-make pizzas. Chopped fresh spinach, sliced black or green olives, or a little crushed pineapple are all great additions.

Pick-Me-Up Mini Pizzas

Chapter Six

Comforting Casseroles

Set the table and get ready for some comforting casseroles that are bound to please. For a one-pan dinner they are sure to love, try Hurry-Up Italian Casserole (chock-full of veggies) or hearty Sausage & Potato Casserole. Want to serve a side dish that will impress them? Stir up Aunt Fran's Cheddar Potatoes or Sugared Sweet Potatoes...both recipes are delicious, yet quick & easy. It is time for dinner and you have the perfect one-pan recipes waiting for everyone to enjoy.

Marie Buche, *Yakima, WA*

Hamburger Pie

With a family of six on a ministry budget, this easy, affordable recipe became the first dinner I taught my three daughters and my son to prepare. Even the leftovers are tasty! This is also my most-requested church potluck recipe. Serve with cinnamon-spiced applesauce for a wonderful family dinner.

Makes 12 servings

2 lbs. ground beef
1 onion, chopped
2 10 ¾-oz. cans tomato soup
28-oz. can green beans, drained
salt and pepper to taste
1 c. shredded Cheddar cheese

Brown beef and onion together in a skillet; drain. Mix soup and beans in a lightly greased 13"x9" baking pan. Stir in beef mixture, salt and pepper; set aside. Spread Potato Topping evenly over mixture in pan; sprinkle with cheese. Bake, uncovered, at 350 degrees for about 30 minutes.

POTATO TOPPING:
3 c. milk
3 c. water
¼ c. butter
1 t. salt
4 c. instant mashed potato
   flakes

Bring all ingredients except potato flakes to a boil. Stir in potato flakes; mix well. Cover and let stand for 5 minutes. If potatoes are too thick to spread, add milk or water to desired consistency.

Hamburger Pie

April King, *Eugene, OR*

Friendship Casserole

This makes a big recipe to share with friends!

Serves 10 to 12

½ c. butter
10 eggs
½ c. all-purpose flour
1 t. baking powder
⅛ t. salt
7-oz. can chopped green chiles
16-oz. container cottage cheese
2 8-oz. pkgs. shredded Monterey Jack cheese

Melt butter in a 13"x9" baking pan, spreading evenly. Beat eggs in a large bowl; stir in flour, baking powder and salt until well blended. Add melted butter and remaining ingredients; mix just until blended. Pour into pan and bake, uncovered, at 400 degrees for 15 minutes; reduce temperature to 350 degrees. Bake for an additional 35 to 40 minutes. Cut into squares and serve hot.

Patricia Rozzelle, *Mineral Bluff, GA*

Sugared Sweet Potatoes

This hearty side dish casserole is sure to become a favorite for any holiday or comfort food dinner.

Makes 10 to 12 servings

1 c. brown sugar, packed
¼ c. butter
¾ t. salt
1 t. vanilla extract
1 c. cola
9 sweet potatoes, boiled and sliced
½ c. chopped pecans

In a medium saucepan, stir together brown sugar, butter, salt, vanilla and cola; bring to a boil for 5 minutes. Arrange potatoes in an ungreased 13"x9" baking pan. Pour brown sugar mixture over potatoes. Sprinkle pecans on top. Bake, uncovered, at 350 degrees for 25 to 30 minutes, until edges are crisp.

Sugared Sweet Potatoes

Shelba Durston, *Lidi, CA*

Baked Italian Sausage Dressing

This is an adaptation of a friend's mom's recipe. She had brought it here from Italy over 60 years ago, and it was written in Italian by her grandmother. I do not speak or read Italian, but I watched what they did in the kitchen and made it my way! We actually begin snacking on this as soon as it is assembled, but it does taste better after baking.

Makes 6 to 8 servings

4 c. sourdough bread cubes
1 lb. sweet or spicy Italian
   ground pork sausage
2 c. fennel bulb, cut into
   ½-inch cubes
2 c. Swiss chard, ribs removed,
   diced and packed
1 sweet onion, chopped
1 c. celery, diced
2 to 4 cloves garlic, pressed,
   to taste
2 c. chicken broth

Spread bread cubes on baking sheets to dry ahead of time. Meanwhile, brown sausage in a large skillet over medium heat until about half cooked. Add vegetables and garlic; cook and stir just until tender. Drain; add bread cubes and toss to mix. Add chicken broth to desired consistency; transfer mixture to a greased 13"x9" baking pan or 3-quart casserole dish. Cover and bake at 350 degrees for 30 minutes, or until heated through.

~ Quick Tip ~

Fennel bulb may be a new ingredient to some cooks, but it is really quite easy to use. The bulb, stalks and fronds of fennel are all edible. The bulb is firm and cuts similar to a raw beet.

Baked Italian Sausage Dressing

Julie Sibbersen, *Portage, MI*

Speedy Ham & Beans

Using instant rice and chopped ham is what makes this dish so speedy to make!

Makes 4 to 6 servings

1 1/3 c. cooked instant rice
14-oz. can green beans, drained
5-oz. can chopped ham
1/3 c. mayonnaise
1 t. chicken bouillon granules
1 1/3 c. boiling water
1 T. dried, minced onion
1/2 c. shredded Cheddar cheese

Combine rice, green beans, ham and mayonnaise in a lightly greased 13"x9" baking pan; set aside. Dissolve bouillon in water; pour over rice mixture. Sprinkle with minced onion and mix well. Bake at 400 degrees for 15 minutes; sprinkle with cheese and bake an additional 5 minutes, or until cheese is melted.

Michelle Powell, *Valley, AL*

Scalloped Sweet Potatoes & Apples

This casserole is a perfect fall addition to any meal. Top with a handful of chopped pecans for extra crunch, if you like. Great with ham!

Makes 6 servings

2 sweet potatoes, boiled, peeled and sliced
2 tart apples, peeled, cored and sliced
1/2 c. brown sugar, packed
1/4 butter, sliced
1 t. salt

Layer half the sweet potatoes in a buttered 13"x9" baking pan. Layer half the apple slices. Sprinkle with half the sugar; dot with half the butter. Repeat with remaining ingredients. Bake, uncovered, at 350 degrees for one hour.

Scalloped Sweet Potatoes & Apples

Jeff Howell, *Minonk, IL*

Turkey Day Leftovers Casserole

I came up with this the day after Thanksgiving when we had lots of leftovers. Add a dish of cranberry sauce on the side.

Makes 6 to 8 servings

3 c. cooked stuffing, or 6-oz.
   pkg. chicken stuffing mix,
   prepared
2 to 3 c. cooked turkey, chopped
   or shredded
1½ to 2 c. turkey gravy
2 c. green bean casserole or
   cooked green beans
4 c. mashed potatoes
2 eggs, beaten
¼ c. milk
1 c. biscuit baking mix
Garnish: shredded Swiss
   cheese

Spread stuffing evenly in a 13"x9" baking pan sprayed with non-stick vegetable spray. Layer turkey over stuffing; spoon gravy over turkey. Layer with green beans and mashed potatoes; set aside. In a bowl, stir together eggs, milk and biscuit mix; spread batter evenly over potatoes. Sprinkle with cheese. Bake, uncovered, at 400 degrees for 30 to 35 minutes, until hot and cheese is melted.

⌣ Quick Tip ⌣

Using leftovers wisely saves time and money. When you find you have leftover soup, ladle 2-cup portions into freezer bags. Seal, label and freeze. Just reheat when you need a quick-fix meal.

Turkey Day Leftovers Casserole

Marlene Campbell, *Millinocket, ME*

Aunt Fran's Cheddar Potatoes

This recipe is shared in memory of my mom, who passed away in 2015. Such a wonderful cook herself, Mom always loved her sister Fran's potato casserole and enjoyed serving it as a special treat for holiday meals.

Makes 6 servings

6 potatoes, peeled and cubed
8-oz. pkg. shredded Cheddar
   cheese
¼ c. butter
1½ c. sour cream
⅓ c. onion, minced
¼ t. pepper
Garnish: 3 T. fresh cilantro,
   chopped

In a large saucepan, cover potatoes with water. Bring to a boil over high heat. Cook until potatoes are fork-tender; drain. In another saucepan over very low heat, melt together cheese and butter, stirring often. Stir in sour cream, onion and pepper; fold in potatoes. Spoon mixture into a 3-quart casserole dish or 13"x9" baking pan sprayed with non-stick vegetable spray. Bake, uncovered, at 350 degrees for 30 to 35 minutes, until bubbly and golden. Garnish with fresh cilantro.

~ **Quick Tip** ~

If you are trying to limit fat and calories, you can substitute plain yogurt for sour cream in almost any recipe.

Aunt Fran's Cheddar Potatoes

Megan Heep, *Chicago, IL*

Sausage & Potato Casserole

This is a great dish to take to a church potluck. It holds well and everyone loves it.

Makes 8 to 10 servings

¼ c. oil
½ c. all-purpose flour
2 t. salt
¼ t. pepper
4 c. milk
8 to 10 potatoes, peeled, cooked and sliced
1 lb. ground sausage, browned and drained
1 c. shredded American cheese

Combine oil, flour, salt and pepper in a large skillet. Cook and stir over medium heat until hot. Whisk in milk, stirring constantly, until thickened; remove from heat. Layer half of potatoes, flour mixture and sausage into an ungreased 13"x9" baking pan; repeat layers. Sprinkle cheese on top. Bake, uncovered, at 350 degrees for 30 minutes, or until cheese begins to brown slightly.

Tiffani Schulte, *Wyandotte, MI*

Blue-Ribbon Corn Dog Bake

This casserole is oh-so easy and it really does taste like a county fair corn dog! Bake it in a cast-iron baking pan to get the edges crisp and golden.

Serves 8 to 10

⅓ c. sugar
1 egg, beaten
1 c. all-purpose flour
¾ T. baking powder
½ t. salt
½ c. yellow cornmeal
½ T. butter, melted
¾ c. milk
16-oz. pkg. fully-cooked hot dogs, grilled
   if desired

In a small bowl, mix together sugar and egg. In a separate bowl, mix together flour, baking powder and salt. Add flour mixture to sugar mixture. Add cornmeal, butter and milk, stirring just to combine. Pour into a well-greased 13"x9" baking pan. Lay hot dogs on top of batter. Bake, uncovered, at 375 degrees for about 15 minutes, until a toothpick inserted near the center comes out clean.

Blue-Ribbon Corn Dog Bake

Tina Knotts, *Marysville, OH*

Cornbread Corn Casserole

The texture of this casserole is so moist and the flavor is so rich. If you have fresh corn, stir in a cup of cooked corn before baking. It gives it even more yummy texture and flavor.

Makes 15 to 18 servings

8½-oz. pkg. corn muffin mix
2 15-oz. cans creamed corn
1 egg, beaten
⅓ c. butter, melted
¾ c. sour cream

Combine ingredients together; pour into a greased 13"x9" baking pan. Bake at 375 degrees for 35 to 45 minutes. Serve warm.

Geneva Rogers, *Gillette, WY*

Roasted Root Vegetables

Roasting brings out the natural sweetness of these beautiful veggies.

Makes 8 servings

2 turnips, peeled and quartered
2 parsnips, peeled and cut into one-inch slices
2 carrots, peeled and thickly sliced
1 yam, peeled and cut into one-inch slices
12 pearl onions, peeled
3 medium beets, peeled and quartered
3 cloves garlic
3 T. olive oil
2 T. fresh rosemary, chopped
¼ t. pepper

Place all of the ingredients in a large plastic zipping bag. Close bag; turn several times to coat vegetables evenly. Spread mixture in a shallow 13"x9" baking pan. Bake at 425 degrees for one hour, stirring once.

Roasted Root Vegetables

Cathy Webster, *Poughkeepsie, NY*

Scalloped Potatoes with Ham

Everyone loves scalloped potatoes with ham! This version of this classic dish is one of our favorite comfort-food recipes.

Serves 8

1 onion, chopped
1 T. oil
3 cloves garlic, finely chopped
2 sweet potatoes, peeled and
    cut into ¼-inch slices
2 potatoes, peeled and cut into
    ¼-inch slices
½ c. all-purpose flour
1 t. salt
¼ t. pepper
2 c. cooked ham, chopped
1½ c. shredded Gruyère cheese,
    divided
1¾ c. milk
1 T. butter, cut into pieces
Optional: 3 T. fresh cilantro,
    chopped

Sauté onion in oil in a saucepan over medium-high heat 5 minutes, or until tender. Add garlic; cook 30 seconds. Remove from heat and set aside. Place potatoes in a large bowl. Combine flour, salt and pepper; sprinkle over potatoes, tossing to coat. Arrange half of potato mixture in a greased 13"x9" baking pan or 3-quart gratin dish. Top with onion mixture, ham and one cup cheese. Top with remaining potato mixture. Pour milk over potato mixture. Dot with butter; cover with aluminum foil. Bake at 400 degrees for 50 minutes. Uncover, top with remaining cheese and bake 20 more minutes, or until potatoes are tender and cheese is golden. Let stand 10 minutes before serving.

～ **Quick Tip** ～
Chop fresh herbs and keep in small plastic bags
in the freezer to have handy for busy
cooking days.

Scalloped Potatoes with Ham

Narita Roady, *Pryor, OK*

Hurry-Up Italian Casserole

This comfort-food casserole is everyone's favorite and it takes just a few minutes to put together. If you have a family garden, you'll love using that produce in this tasty dish.

Makes 6 servings

3 zucchini, thinly sliced
1 yellow squash, thinly sliced
$\frac{1}{2}$ c. water
1 lb. ground beef
$\frac{1}{2}$ c. onion, chopped
2 cloves garlic, minced
$1\frac{1}{2}$ t. Italian seasoning
$\frac{1}{2}$ t. salt
1 T. olive oil
2 c. fresh spinach, torn
$1\frac{1}{2}$ c. marinara sauce
$1\frac{1}{2}$ c. shredded mozzarella
   cheese

Place zucchini and water in a saucepan over medium heat. Cook until tender, about 5 minutes; drain. Meanwhile, in a skillet over medium heat, brown beef, onion and garlic. Drain; sprinkle with seasonings. Spoon into a 13"x9" baking pan and set aside. Add oil to same skillet; add spinach and stir until wilted. Combine spinach and zucchini; mix well and spread over beef mixture. Spread marinara sauce over top; sprinkle with cheese. Bake, uncovered, at 350 degrees for 20 minutes, or until bubbly and cheese is melted.

> ~ **Quick Tip** ~
> Chop up veggies like zucchini and yellow squash ahead of time and keep in a sealed plastic bag until ready to use later in the day. Add a few drops of lemon juice to keep color fresh.

Hurry-Up Italian Casserole

Carrie Knotts, Kalispell, MT

Spicy Sausage & Chicken Creole

I used this dish to win over my husband and his family while we were dating. He likes his food spicy! Of course, you can use a little less hot pepper sauce if you prefer.

Makes 4 servings

14½-oz. can diced tomatoes
½ c. long-cooking rice, uncooked
½ c. hot water
2 t. hot pepper sauce
¼ t. garlic powder
¼ t. dried oregano
16-oz. pkg. frozen broccoli, corn & red pepper blend, thawed
4 boneless, skinless chicken thighs
½ lb. link Italian pork sausage, cooked and quartered
8-oz. can tomato sauce

Combine tomatoes, rice, water, hot sauce and seasonings in a 13"x9" baking pan. Cover and bake at 375 degrees for 10 minutes. Stir vegetables into tomato mixture; top with chicken and sausage. Pour tomato sauce over top. Bake, covered, at 375 degrees for 40 minutes, or until juices of chicken run clear.

> ~ **Quick Tip** ~
>
> Some cooks prefer chicken thighs over chicken breasts because of the flavor and texture. But either will work in most recipes, with approximate cooking times being the same and if pieces are cut to the same size.

Spicy Sausage & Chicken Creole

Shari Miller, *Hobart, IN*

Cheeseburger & Fries Casserole

What could be easier, and everyone asks for more! If you want a little more kick, add some peppers or a little hot sauce.

Makes 6 to 8 servings

2 lbs. ground beef, browned and drained
10 ¾-oz. can golden mushroom soup
10 ¾-oz. can Cheddar cheese soup
20-oz. pkg. frozen crinkle-cut French fries

Combine ground beef and soups; spread in a greased 13"x9" baking pan. Arrange French fries on top. Bake, uncovered, at 350 degrees for 50 to 55 minutes, until fries are golden.

> ~ **Quick Tip** ~
>
> Dried celery leaves add homestyle flavor to soups and stews. Save the leaves from celery stalks, spread them on a baking sheet and dry slowly in a 180-degree oven for three hours. When they're crisp and dry, store them in a canning jar. The leaves can be crumbled right into a simmering soup pot!

Susan Fracker, *New Concord, OH*

Warm & Wonderful Chicken Salad

It always surprises everyone where they hear that this is a warm chicken salad. But after they try it, they never question it again!

Serves 6 to 8

2 c. cooked chicken, shredded
2 c. celery, diced
1 T. onion, grated
1 c. mayonnaise
½ c. slivered almonds
½ t. lemon juice
1 ½ c. shredded Cheddar cheese, divided
½ c. potato chips, crushed

Mix chicken, celery, onion, mayonnaise, almonds, lemon juice and one cup cheese in a greased 13"x9" baking pan. Top with remaining cheese and chips. Bake, uncovered, at 450 degrees for 15 to 20 minutes, until hot and bubbly.

Warm & Wonderful Chicken Salad

KellyJean Gettelfinger, *Sellersburg, IN*

Taco Hot Bake

This baked taco treat is a hit whether it is a main course or served as a party snack. Top your version of this yummy dish with the garnishes you love most.

Serves 6 to 8

2 lbs. ground beef
2 1¼-oz. pkgs. taco seasoning
   mix
1⅓ c. water
6-oz. pkg. chili cheese corn
   chips
10¾-oz. can Cheddar cheese
   soup
1 c. milk
3 c. shredded mozzarella
   cheese, divided
Garnish: sour cream, shredded
   lettuce, halved cherry
   tomatoes, sliced black olives,
   sliced mushrooms

Brown beef in a large skillet over medium heat; drain. Stir in taco seasoning and water; bring to a boil. Reduce heat to low; simmer for 5 minutes, stirring occasionally. Spread corn chips evenly in a lightly greased 13"x9" baking pan. Spoon beef mixture over chips; set aside. In a saucepan over medium-low heat, stir soup and milk until smooth and heated through. Spoon soup mixture over beef mixture. Top with 2 cups cheese. Bake, uncovered, at 350 degrees for 10 to 15 minutes, until hot and bubbly. Remove from oven; top with remaining cheese. Garnish individual portions with desired toppings.

～ Quick Tip ～
Tomatoes are the major dietary source of the antioxidant lycopene, which has been linked to many health benefits.

Taco Hot Bake

Katja Meyer-Thuerke, *Wattenbek, Germany*

Kohlrabi Gratin

This is a wonderful German recipe that everyone asks for every time we get together.

Serves 4

1½ lbs. kohlrabi, peeled and thinly sliced
¼ c. oil, divided
2¼ c. cooked turkey breast, thinly sliced
salt, pepper and nutmeg to taste
2 onions, diced
1 c. whipping cream
1 c. cream cheese with herbs
½ c. fresh chives, finely chopped
½ c. Gruyère cheese, grated

Cook kohlrabi in boiling salted water for 2 to 3 minutes. Rinse with cold water; drain. Heat 2 tablespoons oil in a saucepan over medium-high heat. Cook turkey until golden; add seasonings to taste. Remove from pan and set aside. To the same skillet, add remaining oil and onions. Sauté until golden. Stir in cream and cream cheese. Season again to taste. Reduce heat to medium; stir in chives. Butter a 13"x9" baking pan and layer alternately kohlrabi and turkey in pan. Pour cream sauce over top; sprinkle with Gruyère cheese. Bake, uncovered, at 350 degrees for about 20 minutes.

Martha Stephens, *Sibley, LA*

Spicy Chicken Casserole

A hearty, creamy dinner in one dish...with just four ingredients!

Serves 6

4 to 5 boneless, skinless chicken breasts
2 10¾-oz. cans cream of chicken soup
2 10¾-oz. cans nacho cheese soup
3 to 4 c. tortilla chips, crushed and divided

Cover chicken breasts with water in a large saucepan. Simmer over medium-high heat just until cooked through. Drain, saving broth for another use. Cool chicken slightly; shred into bite-size pieces, and set aside. Combine soups in another saucepan. Stir well; cook over medium heat until bubbly. Remove from heat. In a greased 13"x9" baking pan, layer half of chicken, half of soup mixture and half of the crushed chips. Repeat layers. Cover and bake at 350 degrees for 20 minutes, or until heated through.

Spicy Chicken Casserole

Shirley Gist, *Zanesville, OH*

Turkey Tetrazzini

This tasty casserole is our family's favorite way to enjoy leftover holiday turkey. It's easy to toss together, too.

Makes 6 servings

8-oz. pkg. thin spaghetti, uncooked
2 cubes chicken bouillon
2 to 3 T. dried, minced onion
2 10 ¾-oz. cans cream of mushroom soup
8-oz. container sour cream
½ c. milk
salt and pepper to taste
2 c. cooked turkey, cubed
8-oz. can sliced mushrooms, drained
8-oz. pkg. shredded Cheddar cheese

Cook spaghetti according to package directions, adding bouillon and onion to cooking water. Drain and place in a large bowl. Stir together soup, sour cream, milk, salt and pepper in a medium bowl; fold in turkey and mushrooms. Lightly stir mixture into spaghetti, coating well. Pour into a lightly greased 13"x9" baking pan; top with cheese. Bake at 350 degrees for 30 to 40 minutes, until hot and bubbly.

Gerri Bowers, *Farwell, TX*

Chile Relleno Casserole

My mom served this Chile Relleno Casserole when I was a child, and I've always loved it. Serve it with Spanish rice and refried beans... yum!

Makes 8 servings

16-oz. pkg. shredded Monterey Jack cheese
16-oz. pkg. shredded Cheddar cheese
2 8-oz. cans whole green chiles
4 eggs, separated
1 T. all-purpose flour
⅔ c. evaporated milk
salt and pepper to taste

Sprinkle both packages of cheese into a lightly greased 13"x9" baking pan. Arrange chiles over cheese; set aside. Beat egg yolks in a bowl; gradually beat in flour and milk. In a separate bowl, beat egg whites until fluffy; stir into yolk mixture. Add salt and pepper to taste. Drizzle egg mixture over chiles. Bake, uncovered, at 325 degrees for 50 minutes. Let stand several minutes before serving.

Chile Relleno Casserole

Dave Slyh, *Galloway, OH*

Tangy Corn Casserole

Great for brunch and casual celebrations, this side dish gets a little kick from a dab of hot sauce.

Serves 8

19-oz. pkg. frozen corn, thawed and drained
½ c. onion, chopped
½ c. green pepper, sliced into strips
¾ c. water
1 c. yellow squash, chopped
1 tomato, chopped
1 c. shredded Cheddar cheese, divided
1 c. cornmeal
½ c. milk
3 eggs, beaten
¾ t. salt
¼ t. pepper
¼ t. hot pepper sauce

Combine corn, onion, green pepper and water in a medium saucepan. Bring to a boil; reduce heat to medium-low. Cover and simmer 5 minutes, or until vegetables are crisp-tender. Do not drain. Combine squash, tomato, ¾ cup cheese, cornmeal, milk, eggs, salt, pepper and hot pepper sauce in a large mixing bowl. Add corn mixture to cornmeal mixture; stir to blend. Pour into a greased 13"x9" baking pan. Bake, uncovered, at 350 degrees for 45 to 50 minutes, until heated through. Top with remaining cheese.

Kathy Dassel, *Newburgh, IN*

Savory Rice Casserole

My sister-in-law gave me this delicious recipe while we were visiting her in Raleigh, North Carolina.

Serves 6 to 8

2 4-oz. cans sliced mushrooms, drained and liquid reserved
2 8-oz. cans sliced water chestnuts, drained and liquid reserved
1 c. butter
2 c. long-cooking rice, uncooked
2 10½-oz. cans French onion soup

In a skillet over medium heat, sauté mushrooms and water chestnuts in butter; set aside. Add uncooked rice to an ungreased 3-quart casserole dish or 13"x9" baking pan. Stir in soup, mushroom mixture and reserved liquids. Bake, covered, at 375 degrees for 45 to 60 minutes, until rice is tender.

Savory Rice Casserole

Dawn Romero, *Lewisville, TX*

Sweet Potato Casserole

The coconut and pecans add a special texture and flavor to this amazing sweet potato casserole.

Serves 4

4 c. mashed sweet potatoes
⅓ c. plus 2 T. butter, melted and divided
2 T. sugar
2 eggs, beaten
½ c. milk
⅓ c. chopped pecans
⅓ c. sweetened flaked coconut
⅓ c. brown sugar, packed
2 T. all-purpose flour

In a large bowl, mix together sweet potatoes, ⅓ cup butter and sugar. Stir in eggs and milk.

Spoon mixture into a lightly greased 3-quart casserole dish or 13"x9" baking pan. In a separate bowl, combine remaining butter and other ingredients. Sprinkle mixture over sweet potatoes. Bake, uncovered, at 325 degrees for one hour, or until heated through and bubbly.

Samantha Fishkin, *Lauderdale Lakes, FL*

Mom's Chicken Casserole

This dish just couldn't be easier to make! It only has 3 ingredients but it is always a hit at our family gatherings. Use fresh tomatoes if you have them.

Serves 4 to 6

6-oz. pkg. rice pilaf mix, uncooked
4 to 6 boneless, skinless chicken breasts
2 c. stewed tomatoes

Prepare rice pilaf according to package directions, cooking for just half the time. Transfer pilaf to a greased 13"x9" baking pan. Place chicken breasts over pilaf. Spoon tomatoes over chicken. Bake, covered with aluminum foil, at 350 degrees for one hour, or until chicken juices run clear and all liquid is absorbed.

Mom's Chicken Casserole

Mary Ellen Dawson, *Boise, ID*

Sweet Corn & Rice Casserole

Roll up leftovers in a flour tortilla for a hearty snack.

Serves 10 to 12

2 T. butter
1 green pepper, chopped
1 onion, chopped
15½-oz. can creamed corn
11-oz. can sweet corn & diced
   peppers, drained
11-oz. can corn, drained
6 c. cooked rice
10-oz. can diced tomatoes with
   green chiles, drained
8-oz. pkg. mild Mexican pasteurized
   process cheese spread, cubed
½ t. salt
¼ t. pepper
½ c. shredded Cheddar cheese

Melt butter in a large skillet over medium heat. Add green pepper and onion; sauté 5 minutes, or until tender. Stir in remaining ingredients except shredded cheese; spoon into a lightly greased 13"x9" baking pan. Bake, uncovered, at 350 degrees for 25 to 30 minutes, until heated through. Top with shredded cheese; bake an additional 5 minutes, or until cheese melts.

Sonna Axon Johnson, *Goldfield, IA*

Tuna Noodle Casserole

This classic tuna casserole recipe is our family favorite. Serve with fresh fruit for a complete and filling meal. I also like to take this to our church potlucks...everyone always knows that I brought it and they go right for it!

Serves 6

16-oz. pkg. wide egg noodles, cooked
10 ¾-oz. can cream of mushroom soup
6-oz. can tuna, drained
1 c. frozen peas, thawed
4-oz. can sliced mushrooms, drained
1 c. milk
salt and pepper to taste
1 c. shredded Cheddar cheese

Combine noodles, soup, tuna, peas and mushrooms; stir in milk. Add salt and pepper to taste. Spread in a lightly greased 13"x9" baking pan; sprinkle with cheese. Bake, uncovered, at 350 degrees for 25 minutes, until hot and bubbly.

Tuna Noodle Casserole

Deborah Clouser, McLean, VA

Creamy Chicken & Biscuits

You can see the smiles on the faces of my entire family when I take this dish out of the oven. It doesn't take long to make and it is so good!

Serves 8

2 c. new redskin potatoes,
    halved or quartered
2 c. carrots, peeled and sliced
1 onion, diced
3 T. butter
3 T. all-purpose flour
salt and pepper to taste
2 c. milk
1 c. chicken broth
2 cubes chicken bouillon
2 boneless, skinless chicken
    breasts, cooked and diced
12-oz. tube refrigerated large
    biscuits, cut into quarters

Cover potatoes, carrots and onion with water in a medium saucepan. Bring to a boil over medium heat; reduce heat and simmer until tender. Drain and set aside. Melt butter in another medium saucepan; stir in flour, salt and pepper, stirring constantly. Gradually add milk, broth and bouillon. Cook until thickened, about 3 to 5 minutes; set aside. Combine chicken and vegetables in a lightly greased 13"x9" baking pan. Pour sauce over top; arrange biscuits over sauce. Bake, uncovered, at 400 degrees for 15 minutes, or until biscuits are golden and sauce is bubbly.

> ～ **Quick Tip** ～
> Serve this gravy-rich dish in deep bowls on a contrasting color plate. It will look as beautiful as it tastes.

Creamy Chicken & Biscuits

Jo Ann, Gooseberry Patch

Party Paella Casserole

Here's a great use for rotisserie chicken, shrimp and yellow rice. We like to serve this on New Year's Eve or at our Super Bowl party.

Serves 8

2 8-oz. pkgs. yellow rice, uncooked
1 lb. medium shrimp, cleaned
1 T. fresh lemon juice
½ t. salt
¼ t. pepper
2 cloves garlic, minced
1½ T. olive oil
2½-lb. deli rotisserie lemon-and-garlic chicken, coarsely shredded
5 green onions, chopped
8-oz. container sour cream
1 c. frozen English peas, thawed
1 c. green olives with pimentos, coarsely chopped
1½ c. shredded Monterey Jack cheese
½ t. smoked Spanish paprika

Prepare rice according to package directions. Remove from heat and let cool 30 minutes; fluff with a fork. Meanwhile, toss shrimp with lemon juice, salt and pepper in a bowl. Sauté seasoned shrimp and garlic in hot oil in a large non-stick skillet 2 minutes, or just until done. Remove from heat. Combine shredded chicken, rice, green onions, sour cream and peas in a large bowl; toss well. Add shrimp and olives, tossing gently. Spoon rice mixture into a greased 13"x9" baking pan. Combine cheese and paprika, tossing well; sprinkle over casserole. Bake, uncovered, at 400 degrees for 15 minutes, or just until cheese is melted and casserole is thoroughly heated.

> ～ **Quick Tip** ～
> If you don't have fresh garlic, minced garlic in a jar will do. Simply add the garlic to the meat mixture. One clove of fresh garlic is about the same as 1/2 teaspoon of minced garlic.

Party Paella Casserole

Jill Ross, *Pickerington, OH*

Kale & Potato Casserole

Warm potatoes, wilted greens and Parmesan cheese make this a hearty side!

Serves 4 to 6

½ c. butter, melted
6 potatoes, thinly sliced
15 leaves fresh kale, finely chopped
½ c. grated Parmesan cheese
salt and pepper to taste

Drizzle melted butter over potatoes in a bowl; mix well. In a greased 13"x9" baking pan, layer ⅓ each of potatoes, kale and Parmesan cheese; season with s alt and pepper. Continue layering and seasoning, ending with cheese. Cover and transfer to oven. Bake at 375 degrees for 30 minutes. Uncover; bake for another 15 to 30 minutes, until potatoes are tender.

Tina Goodpasture, *Meadowview, VA*

Parmesan Scalloped Potatoes

Whether you serve them hot, cold or warm... these are some great scalloped potatoes!

Serves 8

2 lbs. Yukon Gold potatoes, thinly sliced
3 c. whipping cream
¼ c. fresh parsley, chopped
2 cloves garlic, chopped
1½ t. salt
¼ t. pepper
⅓ c. grated Parmesan cheese
Garnish: chopped fresh parsley

Layer potatoes in a lightly greased 3-quart casserole dish or 13"x9" baking pan. In a bowl, stir together remaining ingredients except cheese; pour over potatoes. Bake, uncovered, at 400 degrees for 30 minutes, stirring gently every 10 minutes. Sprinkle with cheese; bake again for about 15 minutes, or until bubbly and golden. Let stand 10 minutes before serving. Garnish with fresh parsley.

Parmesan Scalloped Potatoes

Vickie, *Gooseberry Patch*

Squash Casserole

There's something about a classic vegetable casserole that's impossible to resist. Even picky eaters go back for second helpings!

Serves 8

1½ lbs. yellow squash, cut into ¼-inch slices
1 lb. zucchini, cut into ¼-inch slices
1 sweet onion, chopped
2½ t. salt, divided
1 c. carrots, grated
10¾-oz. can cream of chicken soup
8-oz. container sour cream
8-oz. can water chestnuts, drained and chopped
8-oz. pkg. herb-flavored stuffing mix
½ c. butter, melted

Place squash and zucchini in a Dutch oven. Add chopped onion, 2 teaspoons salt and water to cover. Bring to a boil over medium-high heat and cook 5 minutes; drain well. Stir together carrots, soup, sour cream, water chestnuts and remaining salt in a large bowl; fold in squash mixture. Stir together stuffing mix and melted butter; spoon half of stuffing mixture into bottom of a lightly greased 13"x9" baking pan. Spoon squash mixture over stuffing mixture and top with remaining stuffing mixture. Bake at 350 degrees for 30 to 35 minutes, until bubbly and golden, covering with aluminum foil after 20 to 25 minutes to prevent excessive browning, if necessary. Let stand 10 minutes before serving.

> ⌐ **Quick Tip** ⌐
>
> If you're taking a casserole to a potluck dinner or picnic, keep it toasty by covering the casserole dish with aluminum foil and then wrapping it in several layers of newspaper.

Squash Casserole

Trish McGregor, *Prospect, VA*

Buffalo Chicken Quinoa Casserole

If you like buffalo chicken wings, you'll love this casserole.

Serves 8

1 c. quinoa, uncooked
3 c. shredded Cheddar cheese, divided
1 c. buffalo wing sauce, divided
1 c. sour cream
1/4 c. butter, softened
1/4 c. milk
1/2 t. garlic salt
1/4 t. pepper
1 t. dried basil
4 boneless, skinless chicken breasts, cooked
    and cubed

Cook quinoa according to package directions. Meanwhile, in a large bowl, combine 2 cups cheese and 1/2 cup buffalo wing sauce with remaining ingredients except chicken and quinoa. Fold in quinoa. Spread mixture into a greased 13"x9" baking pan. Top with chicken. Drizzle with remaining buffalo wing sauce and sprinkle with remaining cheese. Bake, covered, at 350 degrees for 45 minutes, or until heated through and bubbly.

Anne Marie Verdiramo, *Rochester, MN*

Mushroom & Barley Casserole

This combination of the earthy mushrooms, rich barley and the crunchy slivered almonds is just amazing. My large family loves this recipe! It has even been published in my grandmother's church cookbook.

Serves 4 to 6

1 1/2 c. quick-cooking barley, uncooked
1/2 c. onion, chopped
1/2 c. butter
2 4-oz. can sliced mushrooms
2 14 1/2-oz. cans chicken broth
1 c. slivered almonds

In a saucepan, sauté barley and onion in butter until golden; spoon into a greased 3 quart casserole dish or 13"x9" baking pan. Add undrained mushrooms and broth; mix well. Bake, covered, at 350 degrees for one hour and 15 minutes. Remove cover and sprinkle with almonds. Bake, uncovered, for an additional 15 minutes.

Mushroom & Barley Casserole

Jo Ann, *Gooseberry Patch*

Mexican Veggie Bake

Layers of tasty sautéed fresh vegetables and melted cheese...perfect for a meatless Monday.

Makes 6 servings

½ c. green pepper, finely chopped
½ c. carrot, peeled and finely chopped
½ c. celery, finely chopped
½ c. onion, finely chopped
2 c. cooked rice
16-oz. can refried beans
15-oz. can black beans, drained and rinsed
1 c. salsa
12-oz. pkg. shredded Cheddar cheese, divided

Sauté vegetables in a lightly greased skillet over medium heat until tender, about 5 minutes. Transfer vegetables to a large bowl; add remaining ingredients except cheese. Layer half of mixture in a lightly greased 13"x9" baking pan; sprinkle with half of cheese. Repeat layering, ending with cheese. Bake, uncovered, at 350 degrees until heated through, about 15 to 20 minutes.

Melanie Springer, *Canton, OH*

Broccoli-Corn Casserole

My mom used to make this tasty side dish for holiday dinners. It is a favorite of all who try it. I make it, my kids make it and I have shared this recipe with so many people.

Serves 4

2 10-oz. pkgs. frozen chopped broccoli, thawed and squeezed dry
2 16-oz. cans creamed corn
2 eggs, beaten
1 T. minced dried onion
salt and pepper to taste
½ c. butter, melted and divided
30 saltine crackers, coarsely crushed and divided

In a bowl, combine broccoli, creamed corn, eggs, onion, seasonings, 3 tablespoons melted butter and ⅔ of cracker crumbs. Mix well; transfer to a greased 13"x9" baking pan. In a small bowl, toss together remaining cracker crumbs and butter; sprinkle over casserole. Bake, uncovered, at 350 degrees for about 50 minutes.

Broccoli-Corn Casserole

Wendy Bush, *Morrill, NE*

Easy Carrot Casserole

Makes 6 to 8 servings

4 to 5 carrots, peeled and chopped
1 c. pasteurized process cheese spread, cubed
¼ c. butter
½ onion, finely chopped
¾ c. potato chips, crushed

In a medium saucepan, cook carrots in salted water about 12 minutes; drain. Stir in cheese, butter and onion. Place mixture into a 3-quart casserole dish or 13"x9" baking pan coated with non-stick vegetable spray; top with potato chips. Bake, uncovered, at 350 degrees for 30 minutes.

Valerie Hendrickson, *Cedar Springs, MI*

Mom's Cheesy Hashbrowns

My mother used to make this scrumptious dish the old-fashioned way, starting with hand-shredded boiled potatoes. This version is simplified using frozen shredded potatoes, yet is still full of hearty homestyle flavor!

Serves 6 to 8

¼ c. butter
1 sweet onion, chopped
2 c. shredded Cheddar cheese
1 c. sour cream
30-oz. pkg. country-style frozen shredded hashbrowns, thawed

Melt butter in a medium saucepan over medium heat. Add onion and cook until translucent, about 5 minutes. Mix in cheese and continue stirring until melted. Remove from heat; stir in sour cream. Gently fold mixture into hashbrowns. Spoon into a greased 3-quart casserole dish or 13"x9" baking pan. Bake, uncovered, at 350 degrees for 60 to 75 minutes, until heated through and top is golden.

Mom's Cheesy Hashbrowns

Linda Karner, *Pisgah Forest, NC*

Pork Chop Au Gratin

You'll love this casserole recipe...you have your entire dinner in one pan!

Makes 6 to 8 servings

6 to 8 pork chops
1 t. salt
1 to 2 T. oil
2 c. water
2 carrots, peeled and thinly sliced
10-oz. pkg. frozen Italian green beans
2 T. butter
7-oz. pkg. au gratin potato mix
10¾-oz. can cream of celery soup
⅔ c. milk
2 T. Dijon mustard
½ t. dried basil
½ t. Worcestershire sauce

Sprinkle pork chops with salt. Brown in oil in a skillet over medium heat; set aside. Heat water to boiling in a saucepan; add carrots and beans. Return to a boil; stir in butter, potato slices and sauce from mix. Remove from heat and set aside. Mix soup, milk, mustard, basil and Worcestershire sauce; stir into vegetable mixture and pour into an ungreased 3-quart casserole dish or 13"x9" baking pan. Arrange chops on top. Cover and bake at 350 degrees for 45 minutes; uncover and bake an additional 15 minutes, or until chops are tender. Let stand 5 minutes before serving.

Donna Maltman, *Toledo, OH*

Family-Favorite Corn Soufflé

This is an absolute must-have for Thanksgiving dinner. You can mix it up the night before and pop it in the oven the next morning. So easy!

Serves 8 to 10

15-oz. can corn, drained
8½-oz. pkg. cornbread mix
14¾-oz. can creamed corn
1 c. sour cream
¼ c. butter, melted
8-oz. pkg. shredded Cheddar cheese

Combine all ingredients except cheese. Pour into a lightly greased 13"x9" baking pan or into 8 lightly greased ramekins. Cover with aluminum foil. Bake at 350 degrees for 30 minutes. Uncover; top with cheese. Return to oven and continue baking until cheese is bubbly and golden, about 15 minutes.

Family-Favorite Corn Soufflé

Barbara Girlardo, *Pittsburgh, PA*

Pork Chops & Biscuit Stuffing

This is a yummy version of chicken and biscuits but using pork. Our family loves it...yours will too!

Makes 6 servings

6 pork chops
1 T. oil
10 ¾-oz. can cream of chicken soup
1 c. celery, diced
1 c. onion, diced
¼ t. pepper
⅛ t. poultry seasoning
1 egg, beaten
12-oz. tube refrigerated biscuits

Brown pork chops in oil in a large skillet over medium heat. Arrange chops in a greased 13"x9" baking pan; set aside. Combine remaining ingredients except biscuits in a mixing bowl; set aside. Using a pizza cutter, cut each biscuit into 8 pieces. Fold into soup mixture and spoon over chops. Bake at 350 degrees for 45 to 55 minutes, until biscuits are golden.

Sue Mary Burford-Smith, *Tulsa, OK*

Green Beans Supreme

This isn't your usual green bean casserole. Loaded with cheese and sour cream, it will be your new favorite!

Serves 4 to 6

1 onion, sliced
1 T. fresh parsley, snipped
3 T. butter, divided
2 T. all-purpose flour
½ t. lemon zest
½ t. salt
⅛ t. pepper
½ c. milk
16-oz. pkg. frozen French-style green beans, thawed
8-oz. container sour cream
½ c. shredded Cheddar cheese
¼ c. soft bread crumbs

Cook onion slices and parsley in 2 tablespoons butter in a saucepan over medium heat about 5 minutes, until onion is tender. Blend in flour, lemon zest, salt and pepper. Stir in milk; cook until thick and bubbly. Add beans and sour cream; heat through. Spoon into an ungreased 3-quart casserole dish or 13"x9" baking pan; sprinkle with cheese. Melt remaining butter and toss with bread crumbs; sprinkle over beans. Broil 3 to 4 inches from heat for 3 minutes, or until golden.

Green Beans Supreme

Pat Griedl, Appleton, WI

Country Veggie Bake

This is an easy dinner to toss together. Just mix and pop it in the oven. We like it with a fruit salad or pineapple chunks and cottage cheese. Served together, you have a complete dinner.

Makes 8 servings

1 T. olive oil
2 carrots, peeled, halved
   lengthwise and sliced
2 onions, chopped
1 to 2 cloves garlic, chopped
1 c. mushrooms, quartered
15-oz. can black beans, drained
   and rinsed
14-oz. can vegetable or chicken
   broth
1 c. frozen corn
½ c. pearled barley, uncooked
¼ c. bulghur wheat, uncooked
⅓ c. fresh parsley, snipped
dried thyme to taste
½ c. shredded Cheddar cheese

Heat oil in a large skillet over medium heat. Sauté carrots and onions until carrots are tender. Stir in garlic and mushrooms; sauté 3 minutes. Combine mixture with remaining ingredients except cheese. Spoon into a greased 3-quart casserole dish or 13"x9" baking pan. Bake, covered, at 350 degrees for one hour, stirring once halfway through baking time. Top with cheese. Cover and let stand 5 minutes, or until cheese melts.

> ### ∼ Quick Tip ∼
> Fresh parsley is an herb that can be used in so many ways. It makes a lovely garnish, but it also adds flavor and color to soups, salads, and breads. It is full of Vitamins K, C and A.

Country Veggie Bake

Shelia Butts, *Creedmoor, NC*

Hashbrown Casserole

Such a creamy, filling side dish and it's so easy to make.

Makes 6 servings

10¾-oz. can cream of chicken soup
8-oz. container sour cream
½ c. butter, melted and divided
2 c. shredded sharp Cheddar cheese
salt and pepper to taste
30-oz. pkg. frozen shredded hashbrowns,
   thawed
1 c. corn flake cereal, crushed

In a bowl, combine soup, sour cream, half the butter, shredded cheese, salt and pepper. Pour mixture into a lightly greased 13"x9" baking pan; top with hashbrowns. Mix corn flake cereal and remaining margarine; spread over hashbrowns. Bake, uncovered, at 350 degrees for 30 minutes, or until hot and bubbly.

Tina George, *El Dorado, AR*

Santa Fe Chicken & Potatoes

This simple recipe is easy to prepare on busy nights when you're pressed for time! It smells so good when it's cooking, and it's easy to double for my large family. My family loves this dish served with sweet cornbread muffins.

Serves 6

4 potatoes, peeled and cut into ¾-inch cubes
1 lb. boneless, skinless chicken breasts, cut
   into ¾-inch cubes
2 T. olive oil
1 c. salsa
1 c. frozen corn
1 c. shredded Cheddar cheese
⅓ c. black olives, sliced

Place potatoes in a microwave-safe dish; add a small amount of water. Cover with plastic wrap; vent and microwave on high for 8 to 10 minutes, until tender. Meanwhile, in a large skillet over high heat, sauté chicken in oil over medium-high heat for 5 minutes. Add potatoes; sauté and toss until potatoes are lightly golden. Stir in salsa and corn. Pour into a greased 13"x9" baking pan casserole dish and top with cheese and olives. Bake at 350 degrees for about 20 minutes, until heated through.

Santa Fe Chicken & Potatoes

Laura Strausberger, *Roswell, GA*

Sunday Chicken & Dressing

Canned soups and stuffing mix makes this a dish you can fix in a few minutes. Use a deli roast chicken if you don't have cooked chicken on hand.

Makes 10 servings

10 3/4-oz. can cream of chicken soup
10 3/4-oz. can cream of celery or cream of
    mushroom soup
1 c. chicken broth
2 1/2 to 3 c. cooked chicken, cubed
2 6-oz. pkgs. chicken flavored stuffing mix,
    prepared

Combine soups and broth in a large bowl; set aside. Place half of chicken in a lightly greased 13"x9" baking pan; top with half of stuffing and half of soup mixture. Repeat layers, ending with soup mixture. Bake, uncovered, at 350 degrees for one hour.

Ashley Causey, *Lumberton, TX*

Quick-Fix Chicken Pot Pie

Here is a comfort-food recipe they are sure to love. And it is so easy to make using biscuit mix and canned soup.

Serves 4

1/2 c. plus 2 T. butter, divided
3 boneless skinless chicken breast, cubed
1 t. garlic powder
1 t. onion powder
1/2 t. dried parsley
1 c. carrots, peeled and thinly sliced
1 c. frozen peas, thawed
10 1/2-oz. can cream of chicken soup
salt and pepper to taste
1 1/2 c. biscuit baking mix
1 c. milk

Melt 2 tablespoons butter in a skillet over medium heat; add chicken. Sprinkle chicken with seasonings; sauté until golden and juices run clear. Transfer chicken to a greased 3-quart casserole dish or 13"x9" baking pan; layer with carrots and peas. In a small bowl, mix soup, broth, salt and pepper; pour over vegetables. In a separate bowl, stir together biscuit mix and milk; spoon over top. Melt remaining butter and drizzle over top. Bake, uncovered, at 350 degrees for 35 to 45 minutes, until topping is firm and golden.

Quick-Fix Chicken Pot Pie

Ginia Johnston, *Greeneville, TN*

Fabulous Baked Potato Casserole

Everyone loves a good baked potato! This casserole will remind you of those delicious loaded potatoes.

Serves 8

6 to 7 potatoes, peeled and cubed
2 c. shredded Cheddar cheese
1 c. mayonnaise
$\frac{1}{2}$ c. sour cream
1 onion, diced
6 slices bacon, crisply cooked and crumbled

In a large saucepan, boil potatoes in water until fork-tender, about 20 minutes; drain and set aside to cool. Combine cheese, mayonnaise, sour cream and onion; mix in potatoes, tossing gently to coat. Spread potato mixture in a buttered 13"x9" baking pan; sprinkle bacon on top. Bake, uncovered, at 350 degrees until golden and bubbly, about 20 to 25 minutes.

John Alexander, *New Britain, CT*

Chicken Kiev Casserole

Using a deli roast chicken makes this recipe a snap to fix. If you have leftover cooked chicken, that works great too.

Serves 6

12-oz. pkg. wide egg noodles, uncooked
$\frac{1}{4}$ c. butter, softened
1 t. garlic powder
1 T. fresh parsley, chopped
1 deli roast chicken, cubed, divided and juices
   reserved (about 3 c.)
2 c. frozen peas, thawed
1 c. whipping cream
paprika to taste
Optional: additional fresh parsley

Cook noodles according to package directions until just tender; drain and set aside. In a bowl, combine butter, garlic powder and parsley. Use one teaspoon of butter mixture to grease a 13"x9" baking pan. Layer half the chicken, half the noodles and all the peas; dot with half the remaining butter mixture. Repeat layers with remaining chicken, noodles and butter mixture. Pour reserved chicken juices and cream over top; sprinkle with paprika. Bake, uncovered, at 350 degrees for 30 minutes, or until hot and bubbly. Sprinkle with parsley, if using.

Chicken Kiev Casserole

Michelle Bogie, *Clio, MI*

Not-So-Stuffed Cabbage

Whether your family thinks they like cooked cabbage or not, this casserole will please them all!

Makes 6 servings

8-oz. can tomato sauce

10 ¾-oz. can tomato soup

1 T. brown sugar, packed

½ c. chicken broth or water

1 lb. ground beef, turkey or pork

1 onion, chopped

1 to 2 T. Worcestershire sauce

garlic powder, seasoning salt and pepper
  to taste

1 head cabbage, chopped and divided

4 potatoes, peeled and cubed

Optional: 1 c. mild salsa

In a bowl, stir together sauce, soup, brown sugar and chicken broth or water; set aside. In a separate large bowl, combine meat, onion, Worcestershire sauce and seasonings; mix gently and set aside. In a greased 3-quart casserole dish or 13"x9" baking pan, layer half each of cabbage and potatoes; crumble in half of meat mixture. Pour half of sauce mixture over the top. Repeat, ending with sauce mixture. If desired, pour salsa over the top. Cover and bake at 350 degrees for one hour. Uncover; bake for an additional 30 minutes.

Kimberly Lyons, *Commerce, TX*

Chicken & Rice Casserole

Great with fresh-baked bread and a green salad.

Serves 6 to 8

2 6.2-oz. pkgs. quick-cooking long-grain and
  wild rice with seasoning packets

4 boneless, skinless chicken breasts, cooked
  and cut into 1-inch cubes

3 10¾-oz. cans cream of mushroom soup

1⅓ c. frozen mixed vegetables, thawed

3 c. water

Gently stir together all ingredients. Spread into an ungreased 13"x9" baking pan. Bake, uncovered, at 350 degrees about 45 minutes, stirring occasionally.

Chicken & Rice Casserole

Linda Stone, Cookeville, TN

Seafood Bisque Casserole

Oodles of seafood in a velvety cream sauce.

Serves 6 to 8

7 T. butter, divided
½ lb. small shrimp, peeled and
    cleaned
½ lb. crabmeat, chopped
½ lb. scallops
1 T. shallots, chopped
10 T. sherry or chicken broth,
    divided
½ t. salt
¼ t. pepper
3 T. all-purpose flour
1½ c. milk
dry bread crumbs
grated Parmesan cheese
Garnish: chopped fresh
    parsley, lemon or lime slices

Melt 4 tablespoons butter in a large skillet over medium heat. Add seafood and shallots; sauté for 5 minutes. Sprinkle with 6 tablespoons sherry or broth, salt and pepper; set aside. Melt remaining butter in a small saucepan; add flour, stirring to thicken. Add milk and remaining sherry; stir until smooth. Combine sauce and seafood mixture and place in a lightly greased 13"x9" baking pan baking pan. Sprinkle with bread crumbs and Parmesan; bake, uncovered, at 400 degrees for 30 minutes. Garnish, as desired.

~ **Quick Tip** ~
Keep slices of lemon or lime in a sealed plastic container in your fridge for a squeeze of citrus or garnish for seafood dishes.

Seafood Bisque Casserole

Chapter Seven

Room for Desserts

Sit back and enjoy some yummy desserts that you can take from oven to table in no time. Nothing could be more lovely than Cora's Jam Cake or a sweet S'mores Cobbler with or without ice cream! Want a little lighter end to your meal? Try Brenda's Fruit Crisp or homestyle Cherry-Pecan Bread Pudding. Love a brownie with a cup of coffee? You'll love Divine Praline Brownies and Fabulous Zucchini Brownies. So find the sweet treat that feeds your needs and enjoy every bite!

Elizabeth Wenk, *Cuyahoga Falls, OH*

Orange-Peach Dump Cake

A different flavor combination for this trusty dessert.

Serves 8 to 10

14¹⁄₂ oz. can peach pie filling, chopped
18-oz. pkg. orange cake mix
2 eggs, beaten
¹⁄₂ c. sour cream

Combine all ingredients in an ungreased 13"x9" baking pan. Mix with a fork until well blended; smooth top. Bake at 350 degrees for 40 to 45 minutes.

Amy Snyder, *White Oak, WV*

Healthy Oatmeal Apple Crisp

This quick recipe almost tastes too good to believe that it's good for you!

Makes 16 servings

6 c. tart apples, peeled, cored and sliced
¹⁄₄ c. frozen apple juice concentrate, thawed
1 t. cinnamon, divided
¹⁄₄ c. butter, softened
1 c. quick-cooking oats, uncooked
¹⁄₄ c. whole-wheat flour
¹⁄₄ c. brown sugar, packed

In a bowl, combine apples, apple juice concentrate and ¹⁄₂ teaspoon cinnamon. Stir until well mixed. Spread in an 13"x9" baking pan sprayed with non-stick vegetable spray. In the same bowl, mix remaining cinnamon and other ingredients until crumbly; sprinkle over apples. Bake, uncovered, at 375 degrees for 40 to 50 minutes, until apples are tender and topping is golden. Serve warm.

Healthy Oatmeal Apple Crisp

Brenda Ervin, *Festus, MO*

Fabulous Zucchini Brownies

The zucchini in these brownies keeps them moist and gives a lovely texture.

Makes 20 servings

1¼ c. sugar
⅓ c. oil
2 t. vanilla extract
2 c. all-purpose flour
½ c. baking cocoa
1 t. baking soda
2 c. zucchini, shredded
½ c. chopped pecans

Mix sugar, oil and vanilla; set aside. In a separate bowl, whisk together flour, cocoa and baking soda. Blend in sugar mixture, zucchini and nuts. Pour into a lightly oiled 13"x9" baking pan and bake at 350 degrees for 25 to 30 minutes. Cut into squares.

Brenda Smith, *Delaware, OH*

Brenda's Fruit Crisp

Here's my favorite dessert recipe...it's a yummy way to use a bumper crop of peaches, apples or berries!

Serves 6

5 c. frozen peaches, apples or berries, thawed and juices reserved
1 T. sugar
½ c. long-cooking oats, uncooked
⅓ c. brown sugar, packed
¼ c. all-purpose flour
¼ t. vanilla extract
¼ t. nutmeg
¼ t. cinnamon
¼ c. unsweetened flaked coconut
⅓ c. butter, diced
Garnish: vanilla ice cream

Place fruit and reserved juices in an ungreased 13"x9" baking pan; stir in sugar and set aside. Mix oats, brown sugar, flour, vanilla and spices in a bowl. Stir in coconut. Add butter to oat mixture; mix with a fork until mixture is the texture of coarse crumbs. Sprinkle over fruit. Bake at 375 degrees for 30 to 35 minutes, until topping is golden and fruit is tender. Serve warm, topped with a scoop of ice cream.

Brenda's Fruit Crisp

Karen Norman, *Jacksonville, FL*

Sweet Mini Apple Dumplings

This is a super easy way to make dumplings and everyone loves them!

Makes 32 dumplings

2 8-oz. tubes refrigerated crescent rolls, separated
4 apples, peeled, cored and sliced into 8 wedges
½ c. butter
1 c. sugar
1 c. water
½ t. cinnamon

Cut each crescent roll in half, forming 2 triangles from each; roll up one apple wedge in each triangle crescent-roll style. Arrange in a 13"x9" baking pan coated with non-stick vegetable spray; set aside. Add butter, sugar and water to a small saucepan; bring to a boil. Reduce heat; boil and stir until sugar dissolves. Pour over crescents; bake at 350 degrees for 30 minutes. Sprinkle with cinnamon.

Carma Brown, *Xenia, OH*

Cora's Jam Cake

My grandmother had this recipe written in a notebook dated 1941. We changed it a bit to make it our own.

Makes 20 servings

2 ½ c. all-purpose flour
⅔ c. butter, melted
1 c. seedless blackberry jam
⅔ c. plain Greek yogurt
2 eggs, beaten
¾ c. sugar
1 t. baking soda
1 t. ground cloves
1 t. cinnamon
1 t. allspice
1 t. nutmeg
Optional: ⅔ c. fresh blackberries
Garnish: powdered sugar, additional fresh blackberries, thyme sprigs

Combine all ingredients except optional blackberries and garnish in a large bowl; mix well. Pour into a greased and floured 13"x9" baking pan. Sprinkle with blackberries if using. Bake at 350 degrees for 25 minutes, or until toothpick inserted in center of cake comes out clean. Garnish as desired.

Cora's Jam Cake

Regina Ferrigno, *Delaware, OH*

Spiced Baked Fruit

Guests "ooh" and "ahh" when they discover the rows of fruit under the pineapple...so pretty!

Serves 6 to 8

16-oz. can apricot halves, drained
16-oz. can pear halves, drained
29-oz. can peach halves, drained
8-oz. can pineapple slices, drained and ½ c.
   juice reserved
⅓ c. brown sugar, packed
1 T. butter
½ t. cinnamon
¼ t. ground cloves

In a greased 13"x9" baking pan, starting at the short end, arrange rows of fruit in the following order: half the apricots, half the pears and half the peaches. Repeat rows. Arrange pineapple over fruit. In a saucepan over medium heat, combine reserved pineapple juice and remaining ingredients. Cook and stir until sugar is dissolved and butter is melted. Pour over fruit. Bake, uncovered, at 350 degrees for 20 to 25 minutes, until heated through.

Jennie Gist, *Gooseberry Patch*

Apple Bread Pudding

Day-old bread is best for soaking up the liquid in this oh-so-decadent dessert.

Serves 12

4 eggs
1½ c. sugar
3 12-oz. cans evaporated milk
½ c. butter, melted
1 T. vanilla extract
2 t. cinnamon
6 c. French bread, torn into pieces and packed
1 Granny Smith apple, peeled, cored and
   chopped
1½ c. walnuts, coarsely chopped and toasted
1 c. golden raisins

Whisk eggs in a large bowl. Whisk in sugar, evaporated milk, melted butter, vanilla and cinnamon. Fold in bread and remaining ingredients, stirring until bread is moistened. Pour into a greased 13"x9" baking pan. Bake, uncovered, at 350 degrees for 50 minutes, or until set. Cut into squares. Serve warm with Rum Sauce.

RUM SAUCE

2 14-oz. cans sweetened condensed milk
2 T. dark rum or 1 t. rum extract
1 T. vanilla extract

Pour condensed milk into a small saucepan; cook over medium heat until hot, stirring often. Remove from heat; stir in rum and vanilla. Serve warm. Makes 2 ½ cups.

Apple Bread Pudding

Shirley Kelly, *Nashua, NH*

Strawberry-Nectarine Cobbler

Make this refreshing cobbler with summer-ripe fruit...yum! Add a scoop of ice cream, if you like.

Makes 12 servings

6 to 8 nectarines, pitted and very thinly sliced
¼ c. light brown sugar, packed
1 t. cinnamon
¼ t. nutmeg
1 t. salt
2 c. fresh strawberries, hulled and halved
2 T. butter, sliced
½ c. sugar, divided
1 egg, beaten
1 T. baking powder
1 c. all-purpose flour
1 T. vanilla extract
½ c. milk

Combine nectarines, brown sugar, spices and salt in a bowl; let stand for 15 minutes. In a saucepan over low heat, combine strawberries, butter and ¼ cup sugar. Cook and stir for 5 minutes, until syrupy. Remove from heat; cool. In another bowl, whisk together egg, remaining sugar, baking powder, flour, vanilla and milk. Spread nectarine mixture evenly in an ungreased 13"x9" glass baking pan. Spoon strawberry mixture evenly over nectarines. Dollop with spoonfuls of batter. Bake at 350 degrees for 30 to 35 minutes. Cool at least 15 minutes before serving.

Barbara Hoover, *Mitchellville, IA*

Barbara's Raspberry Cake

This cake is so light and easy to make. You can use whatever flavor of gelatin you like. It comes together so quickly, but everyone just raves about it!

Serves about 12

16-oz. pkg. white cake mix
3-oz. pkg. raspberry gelatin mix
1 c. boiling water
8-oz. container frozen whipped topping, thawed
Optional: fresh raspberries

Prepare cake mix as instructed on the package. Pour batter into an ungreased 13"x9" glass baking pan. Meanwhile, in another bowl, stir together gelatin mix and boiling water; stir until dissolved. When the cake comes out of the oven, use a fork to poke about 12 holes in the top of the cake and pour the hot gelatin mixture into the holes. Cool in the refrigerator. When cool, top with whipped topping. Decorate as desired. Keep cake refrigerated.

Barbara's Raspberry Cake

Phyllis Cowgill, La Porte, IN

Granny's Apple Coffee Cake

I remember my dear mother and great-grandmother making this cake with apples and butternuts picked right off the tree and fresh milk from our cows. It's called a coffee cake, but we always loved it as a dessert as well with a cup of coffee.

Makes 12 servings

2 c. all-purpose flour
1 c. sugar
3 t. baking powder
1 t. cinnamon
½ t. salt
¾ c. butter, softened
3 eggs, beaten
1 c. milk
3 c. apples, peeled, cored, sliced
   and divided

Combine flour, sugar, baking powder, cinnamon and salt in a bowl; mix well. Blend in butter, eggs and milk; pour half of batter into a greased and floured 13"x9" baking pan. Arrange half of apples over batter; sprinkle with half of the Topping. Arrange remaining apples over Topping, followed by remaining batter and remaining Topping. Bake at 350 degrees for 40 minutes.

TOPPING
½ c. brown sugar, packed
3 T. all-purpose flour
½ c. chopped walnuts
1½ t. cinnamon
1 T. butter

Combine all ingredients in a bowl; mix well.

Granny's Apple Coffee Cake

Jo Ann, *Gooseberry Patch*

JoAnn's Chocolate Bread Pudding

A luscious chocolate dessert that's easy to make. Your guests will love it and so will you!

Makes 8 servings

16-oz. loaf French or Italian
    bread, cubed
3 c. milk
1 c. whipping cream, divided
½ c. coffee-flavored liqueur
1 c. sugar
1 c. light brown sugar, packed
¼ c. baking cocoa
6 eggs, lightly beaten
1 T. vanilla extract
2 t. almond extract
1 ½ t. cinnamon
8-oz. pkg. semi-sweet baking
    chocolate, grated and divided

Spread bread cubes in a lightly greased 13"x9" baking pan; set aside. In a large bowl, whisk together milk, ¼ cup cream and liqueur; set aside. In a separate bowl, combine sugars and cocoa; mix well. Add sugar mixture to milk mixture; stir well. In a small bowl, whisk together eggs, extracts and cinnamon; add to milk mixture and mix well. Reserve a little grated chocolate for garnish; stir in remaining chocolate. Pour mixture over cubed bread. Let stand, stirring occasionally, for about 20 minutes, until bread absorbs most of the milk mixture. Bake at 325 degrees for one hour, or until set and a knife tip inserted in the center tests clean. Whip remaining cream with an electric mixer on high speed until soft peaks form. Serve pudding warm or chilled, garnished with whipped cream and reserved chocolate.

> ~ **Quick Tip** ~
>
> Coffee adds a rich taste to chocolate recipes...
> just substitute an equal amount for water or
> milk in cake, cookie or brownie recipes.

JoAnn's Chocolate Bread Pudding

Arlene Smulski, *Lyons, IL*

Chocolate-Cherry Cobbler

Top with dollops of whipped cream...luscious!

Serves 4 to 6

¼ c. butter, melted
½ t. vanilla extract
30-oz. can cherry pie filling
1 c. all-purpose flour
1 c. sugar
1½ t. baking powder
¼ c. baking cocoa
½ c. milk

In a small bowl, combine melted butter and vanilla; spread mixture in a 13"x9" baking pan. Pour pie filling into pan; set aside. In a bowl, mix together flour, sugar, baking powder and cocoa. Stir in milk. Pour batter over pie filling; do not stir. Bake at 350 degrees for 30 to 40 minutes, until golden. Serve warm.

Kathleen Sturm, *Corona, CA*

Sweet Raspberry-Oat Bars

These layered bars with raspberry jam in the middle are my husband's favorite!

Makes 2 ½ dozen

½ c. butter
1 c. brown sugar, packed
1½ c. all-purpose flour
½ t. baking soda
½ t. salt
1½ c. long-cooking oats, uncooked
¼ c. water
⅔ c. seedless raspberry jam
1 t. lemon juice

In a large bowl, blend together butter and brown sugar until fluffy; set aside. Combine flour, baking soda and salt in a separate bowl. Stir flour mixture into butter mixture. Add oats and water; mix together until crumbly. Firmly pat half of oat mixture into the bottom of a greased 13"x9" baking pan. In a small bowl, stir together jam and lemon juice; spread over oat mixture. Sprinkle remaining oat mixture over top. Bake at 350 degrees for 25 minutes. Cool completely before cutting into bars.

Sweet Raspberry-Oat Bars

Sandy Bernards, *Valencia, CA*

Divine Praline Brownies

These rich and thick brownies are super easy to make and impress everyone who takes a yummy bite!

Makes 12 to 15

22¹/₂-oz. pkg. brownie mix
¹/₄ c. butter
1 c. brown sugar, packed
1 c. chopped pecans

Prepare brownie mix according to package directions. Spread batter in a greased 13"x9" baking pan. Set aside. Melt butter in a skillet over low heat; add brown sugar and pecans. Cook until sugar dissolves; drizzle over brownie batter. Bake at 350 degrees for 25 to 30 minutes. Cool and cut into bars. Keep refrigerated.

Gerry Donnella, *Boston, VA*

Tried & True Apple Casserole

My family loves these easy baked apples.

Serves 8

8 to 10 tart apples, peeled, cored and halved
¹/₂ c. sugar
1 T. all-purpose flour
¹/₂ t. cinnamon
¹/₄ t. nutmeg
1 T. butter, diced
Optional: golden raisins, chopped walnuts

Place apples in a greased 3-quart casserole dish or 13"x9" baking pan; set aside. Mix together dry ingredients; sprinkle over apples. Dot with butter. Sprinkle with raisins and walnuts, if desired. Cover and bake at 350 degrees for 45 minutes to one hour.

Tried & True Apple Casserole

Becky Smith, *North Canton, OH*

Royal Strawberry Shortcake

This classic dessert is still everyone's favorite at our house. We make it for special occasions but also when we feel like we need a little treat.

Makes 12 servings

¼ c. butter
⅓ c. sugar
1 egg, beaten
2 c. all-purpose flour
4 t. baking powder
⅛ t. salt
1 c. skim milk
2 t. vanilla extract
3¾ c. strawberries, hulled and sliced
Garnish: light whipped topping, powdered
    sugar

In a large bowl, blend together butter and sugar. Add egg; mix well. In a separate bowl, combine flour, baking powder and salt. Add flour mixture to butter mixture alternately with milk. Stir in vanilla. Spread batter in a greased 13"x9" baking pan. Bake at 350 degrees for 25 to 30 minutes. Cool; cut shortcake into squares and split. Place bottom layers of shortcake squares on dessert plates. Top with strawberries. Add whipped topping if desired. Add shortcake tops and more berries. Add more whipped topping if desired.

Sharon Demers, *Delores, CO*

Cherry-Pecan Bread Pudding

This old-fashioned bread pudding recipe is one of our favorites.

Serves 12

2-lb. loaf French bread, cubed
6 c. 2% milk
½ c. plus 2 T. sugar, divided
6 eggs, beaten
2 t. vanilla extract
½ t. cinnamon
½ c. dried tart cherries
½ c. chopped pecans
¼ c. butter, melted

Spread bread cubes on a baking sheet; let dry overnight. Combine milk and 5 tablespoons sugar in a saucepan over low heat. Heat to 120 degrees on a candy thermometer; remove from heat. Whisk together eggs, vanilla, cinnamon and remaining sugar in a large bowl. Stir in cherries and pecans. Slowly whisk half of milk mixture into egg mixture; add remaining milk mixture. Stir in bread cubes; toss to mix and let stand for 5 minutes. Mix in butter; transfer mixture to lightly greased 13"x9" baking pan. Bake at 350 degrees for 35 minutes, or until center is firm. Serve warm.

Cherry-Pecan Bread Pudding

Audra Vanhorn-Sorey, *Columbia, NC*

S'mores Cobbler

A unique twist on a family favorite...it's sure to be a hit!

Makes 10 servings

5-oz. pkg. cook & serve
  chocolate pudding mix
1 c. whole milk
6 whole graham crackers,
  broken in half
½ c. mini semi-sweet chocolate
  chips
18½-oz. pkg. chocolate cake
  mix
½ c. butter, sliced
10-oz. pkg. marshmallows

Prepare pudding mix with milk, according to package directions; cool slightly. Spoon pudding into an ungreased 13"x9" baking pan. Arrange graham crackers over pudding, with some space between crackers. Sprinkle with chocolate chips; spread dry cake mix over top and dot with butter. Bake at 350 degrees for 25 minutes. Remove from oven; stir slightly to ensure all ingredients are moistened. Top with marshmallows. Bake for an additional 8 to 10 minutes, until marshmallows are melted.

> ~ **Quick Tip** ~
> For blue-ribbon perfect chocolate cakes with no white streaks, use baking cocoa instead of flour to dust greased pans.

S'mores Cobbler

Judy Lange, *Imperial, PA*

Ginger Ale Baked Apples

A yummy fall dessert or after-the-game snack!

Serves 6

6 baking apples
½ c. golden raisins, divided
6 t. brown sugar, packed and divided
¾ c. ginger ale

Core apples but do not cut through bottoms. Place apples in an ungreased 13"x9" baking pan. Spoon one tablespoon raisins and one teaspoon brown sugar into center of each apple. Pour ginger ale over apples. Bake, uncovered, at 350 degrees, basting occasionally with ginger ale, for 45 minutes, or until apples are tender. Serve warm or cold.

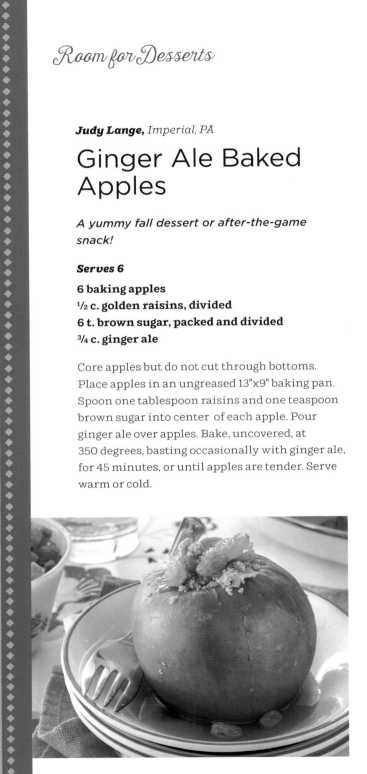

Jennifer Martineau, *Hillard, OH*

Peanut Butter-Oat Bars

I put these bars on the dessert potluck table and everyone loves them!

Makes 2 dozen

½ c. whole-wheat flour
1 t. cinnamon
½ t. baking soda
⅛ t. sea salt
¾ c. crunchy peanut butter
¼ c. brown sugar, packed
⅓ c. honey
1 egg
2 egg whites
2 T. sunflower or olive oil
2 t. vanilla extract
2 c. long-cooking oats, uncooked
1 c. sweetened dried cranberries or raisins
½ c. sliced almonds
½ c. white or dark chocolate chips
Optional: chocolate frosting

Whisk together flour, cinnamon, baking soda and salt in a small bowl. In a separate bowl, beat peanut butter, brown sugar and honey with an electric mixer on medium speed. Beat egg and whites in a separate bowl; add to peanut butter mixture. Mix in oil and vanilla. Add flour mixture; stir in remaining ingredients. Spread into a greased 13"x9" baking pan, using the back of a spatula to spread easily. Bake at 350 degrees for 20 to 25 minutes. Cut into squares. Drizzle with frosting, if desired.

Peanut Butter-Oat Bars

Vickie, Gooseberry Patch

Homemade Carrot Cake

This moist and rich carrot cake has just the right amount of spice, and the nuts add the perfect texture. Your family will love it!

Serves 18

4 eggs, beaten
¾ c. canola oil
½ c. applesauce
1 c. sugar
1 c. brown sugar, packed
1 T. vanilla extract
2 c. all-purpose flour
2 t. baking powder
2 t. baking soda
½ t. salt
1 T. cinnamon
½ t. nutmeg
3 c. carrots, peeled and grated
Optional: ½ c. chopped pecans
Garnish: carrot curls

In a large bowl, beat together eggs, oil, applesauce, sugars and vanilla. Add remaining ingredients except carrots and pecans; mix well. Stir in carrots; fold in pecans if using. Pour into a greased 13"x9" baking pan. Bake at 350 degrees for 40 to 50 minutes, until a toothpick inserted in center comes out clean. Let cool in pan for 10 minutes; turn out onto a wire rack and cool completely. Frost; garnish with carrot curls.

FROSTING

¼ c. butter, softened
8-oz. pkg. cream cheese, softened
2 c. powdered sugar
1 t. vanilla extract

Combine all ingredients in a bowl. Beat until smooth and creamy.

Homemade Carrot Cake

Dianna Oakland, *Titusville, FL*

Dianna's Best Tiramisu

I have tried many versions of this dessert...this one is by far the best. Everyone always asks for seconds and the recipe!

Serves 16 to 24

1 c. brewed coffee, cooled
½ c. plus 1 T. sugar, divided
2 8-oz. pkgs. cream cheese, softened
2 T. almond-flavored liqueur or ½ t. almond extract
12-oz. container frozen whipped topping, thawed
16-oz. pound cake, cut into 30 slices
1 T. baking cocoa

Combine coffee and one tablespoon sugar in a medium bowl; set aside. In a bowl, beat cream cheese with an electric mixer at medium speed, until fluffy. Add remaining sugar and almond liqueur or extract. Gently fold in whipped topping and set aside. Layer 10 cake slices on the bottom of an ungreased 13"x9" baking pan. Brush one-third of coffee mixture over cake slices with a pastry brush. Top with one-third of cream cheese mixture. Repeat 2 more times to create 3 layers. Sprinkle cocoa over top and chill until ready to serve.

Amy Greenlee, *Carterville, IL*

Honey-Baked Bananas

My mom shared this recipe for luscious honeyed bananas. They are so quick to make and always a hit!

Serves 6

6 bananas, halved lengthwise
2 T. butter, melted
¼ c. honey
2 T. lemon juice
Garnish: toasted coconut, lemon slices

Arrange bananas in an ungreased 13"x9" baking pan. Blend remaining ingredients; brush over bananas. Bake, uncovered, at 350 degrees for about 15 minutes, turning occasionally. Garnish with toasted coconut and lemon slices.

Honey-Baked Bananas

Index

Index

U. S. to Metric Recipe Equivalents

Volume Measurements

¼ teaspoon	1 mL
½ teaspoon	2 mL
1 teaspoon	5 mL
1 tablespoon = 3 teaspoons	15 mL
2 tablespoons = 1 fluid ounce	30 mL
¼ cup	60 mL
⅓ cup	75 mL
½ cup = 4 fluid ounces	125 mL
1 cup = 8 fluid ounces	250 mL
2 cups = 1 pint = 16 fluid ounces	500 mL
4 cups = 1 quart	1 L

Weights

1 ounce	30 g
4 ounces	120 g
8 ounces	225 g
16 ounces = 1 pound	450 g

Baking Pan Sizes

Square

8x8x2 inches	2 L = 20x20x5 cm
9x9x2 inches	2.5 L = 23x23x5 cm

Rectangular

13x9x2 inches	3.5 L = 33x23x5 cm

Loaf

9x5x3 inches	2 L = 23x13x7 cm

Round

8x1½ inches	1.2 L = 20x4 cm
9x1½ inches	1.5 L = 23x4 cm

Recipe Abbreviations

t. = teaspoon	ltr. = liter
T. = tablespoon	oz. = ounce
c. = cup	lb. = pound
pt. = pint	doz. = dozen
qt. = quart	pkg. = package
gal. = gallon	env. = envelope

Oven Temperatures

300° F	150° C
325° F	160° C
350° F	180° C
375° F	190° C
400° F	200° C
450° F	230° C

Kitchen Measurements

A pinch = ⅛ tablespoon
1 fluid ounce = 2 tablespoons
3 teaspoons = 1 tablespoon
4 fluid ounces = ½ cup
2 tablespoons = ⅛ cup
8 fluid ounces = 1 cup
4 tablespoons = ¼ cup
16 fluid ounces = 1 pint
8 tablespoons = ½ cup
32 fluid ounces = 1 quart
16 tablespoons = 1 cup
16 ounces net weight = 1 pound
2 cups = 1 pint
4 cups = 1 quart
4 quarts = 1 gallon

Send us your favorite recipe

and the memory that makes it special for you!*

....

If we select your recipe for a brand-new **Gooseberry Patch** cookbook, your name will appear right along with it...and you'll receive a FREE copy of the book!

Submit your recipe on our website at
www.gooseberrypatch.com/sharearecipe

*Please include the number of servings and all other necessary information.

Have a taste for more?

Visit www.gooseberrypatch.com to join our Circle of Friends!

....

- Free recipes, tips and ideas plus a complete cookbook index
- Get mouthwatering recipes and special email offers delivered to your inbox.

From our Kitchen to Yours

You'll also love these cookbooks from **Gooseberry Patch**!

A Year of Holidays

Our Best Cast-Iron Cooking Recipes

Christmas for Sharing

Classic Church Potlucks

Mom's Go-To Recipes

Our Best Blue-Ribbon Recipes

Our Best Recipes from Grandma's Cookie Jar

Quick & Easy Recipes With Help From My
    Kitchen Appliances

Shortcuts to Grandma's Best Recipes

Slow Cooker Casseroles and Skillets

Spring & Summer Recipes for Sharing

Welcome Autumn Cookbook

www.gooseberrypatch.com